Kineton

The Village and its History

Kineton

The Village and its History

A brief history with guided walks round one of Warwickshire's Domesday villages

Kineton and District Local History Group

First published in the United Kingdom in 1999
by
Kineton and District Local History Group

All rights reserved

Text © Kineton and District Local History Group

Mapping based upon Ordnance Survey maps with the permission of the Controller of Her Majesty's Stationery Office
© Crown copyright

ISBN 0 9537004 0 2

British Library Cataloguing in Publication Data
A catalogue record for this book is available from the British Library

Cover design by Design Principles, Kineton

Printed by Warwick Printing Company Limited
Theatre Street, Warwick, CV34 4DR

Contents

List of Illustrations		iv
Preface		vi
Chapter 1	An Introductory History	1

Chapter 2	For the Visitor:
	The Parish Church and Five Walks Round Kineton
	    Walk A - Bridge Street
	    Walk B - Banbury Street and Mill Lane
	    Walk C - Southam Street
	    Walk D - Warwick Road
	    Walk E - Little Kineton
		15

Chapter 3	The Shaping of a Community:
	For those who want to know more
	    The Manor
	    Agriculture and Trades
	    Helping the Poor
	    Schools
	    Fire Services
	    Kineton's Own Gas Company
	    Kineton's Mills
	    The Railway
	    Kineton Green Bus Service
	    The Warwickshire Hunt
		56

Chapter 4	Village Life
	    Mother's Union and WI
	    The Brass Band
	    May Day
	    The Salvation Army
	    Church Choir Outings
	    Flower shows
	    Kyneton, Australia
	    "My Village"
		89

Chapter 5	A Reference File - For Researchers	102
Index		108

List of Illustrations

Frontispiece. The Warwick Road, Kineton.	Facing page 1
The Roman Villa, Brookhampton.	2
The 13th century west doorway of St Peter's Church.	3
The Market Charter.	4
The Kineton Medal.	6
Ridge and furrow.	7
The War Memorial.	10
War work in the Lucas factory.	12
Population growth.	13
St Peter's Church about 1810.	16
A Bentley mermaid in the Parish Church.	17
The Court House, Bridge Street.	18
Outside the Post Office in Bridge Street.	20
John Griffin's grocery shop in Bridge Street.	21
Clarendon House VAD hospital.	22
The Swan Inn, Banbury Street.	26
The Manor Lane bakery.	27
Arthur Rouse's grocery shop, Banbury Street.	28
Osier workers.	31
The Edgehill monument.	32
Kineton from the Banbury Road.	33
Southam Street. The Liberal Club, the Midland Bank and the Central Stores.	35
The 'new' Roman Catholic Church.	36
Southam Street.	37
Blacksmith Jack Walker.	38
Market Square. The Rose and Crown Inn and the school.	40
Pupils at the village school.	42
The Kineton Garage and the Public Hall.	44
The first Police Station in the Warwick Road.	46
The Fire Brigade in the Warwick Road.	47
Kineton Railway Station.	48
The Turnpike milepost on Pittern Hill.	50
Kineton House, Little Kineton.	52
The pond, Little Kineton.	54
Henry Verney, 18th Lord Willoughby de Broke.	57
Little Kineton House in the 18th century.	58

Haymaking.	61
Kineton schoolchildren perform 'the Bean Setting Dance'.	62
A reaper-binder.	63
Vic Wills and his cycle shop in Banbury Street.	65
Josiah Woodley.	68
Joseph Chandler.	70
Diana Lodge, Little Kineton.	72
The Fire Brigade, 1931.	74
The Fire Brigade, 1950.	76
Gas Company share certificate.	77
The Gas Works.	78
The remains of the windmill on Pittern Hill.	80
Gangers working on the line at Kineton Station.	82
Richard Greville Verney, 19th Lord Willoughby de Broke.	84
A Kineton Green bus and its crew.	85
The Warwickshire Hunt meet in Little Kineton.	87
Members of the Women's Institute in 1925.	90
Schoolchildren take the Maypole round the village.	93
St Peter's Church choir in 1892.	96
Kineton from 'Big Field'.	100

Maps

An outline map of Kineton	vii
Kineton - a detailed map	viii-ix
The Market Square	39
Kineton's railway line	83

Acknowledgements

Except where otherwise stated, all illustrations are taken from collections built up by David Beaumont and the Kineton and District Local History Group with the assistance of many local people.

The following illustrations are reproduced by the kind permission of

The Shakespeare Birthplace Trust Records Office	6, 16, 58, 68
The Warwickshire County Record Office	4
The Royal Commission on Historical Monuments Record Centre	2, 3

PREFACE

From the moment of its formation in 1987, Kineton and District Local History Group has wanted to produce a definitive history of its area. This book is not it! The authors are only too well aware that they have not covered any part of the 'district' referred to in the Group's name, and that lack of knowledge has forced them to omit much that they would have liked to include. It is therefore only a first attempt - one which they hope will prove of interest both to long-term residents and to the passing visitor to Kineton. Its aim is to open people's eyes to their rich heritage as they walk round the streets of this ancient community. If it prompts a further search of cupboards and attics for family treasures, then the History Group hopes that future editions, and future readers, will benefit.

This book would not have appeared at all had it not been for the dedicated group of people who have written much of the text and provided most of the photographs, in particular Peter Ashley-Smith, David Beaumont, Peter Holdsworth, Neil Willoughby, and the late Charlie Ivin. They have had admirable support from the members of the History Group, who contributed notes and articles about their special interests. The generous financial support of the Kineton Parish Council and the Warwickshire Rural Community Council has allowed them to produce a more visually appealing, and longer, book than they at first planned.

The authors would also like to thank the staff of the two local record offices, who have advised on research, and produced a never-ending supply of documents and newspapers for them to study.

Throughout the text, references in square brackets [ ] are to map locations on pages vii - ix, or to page 39.

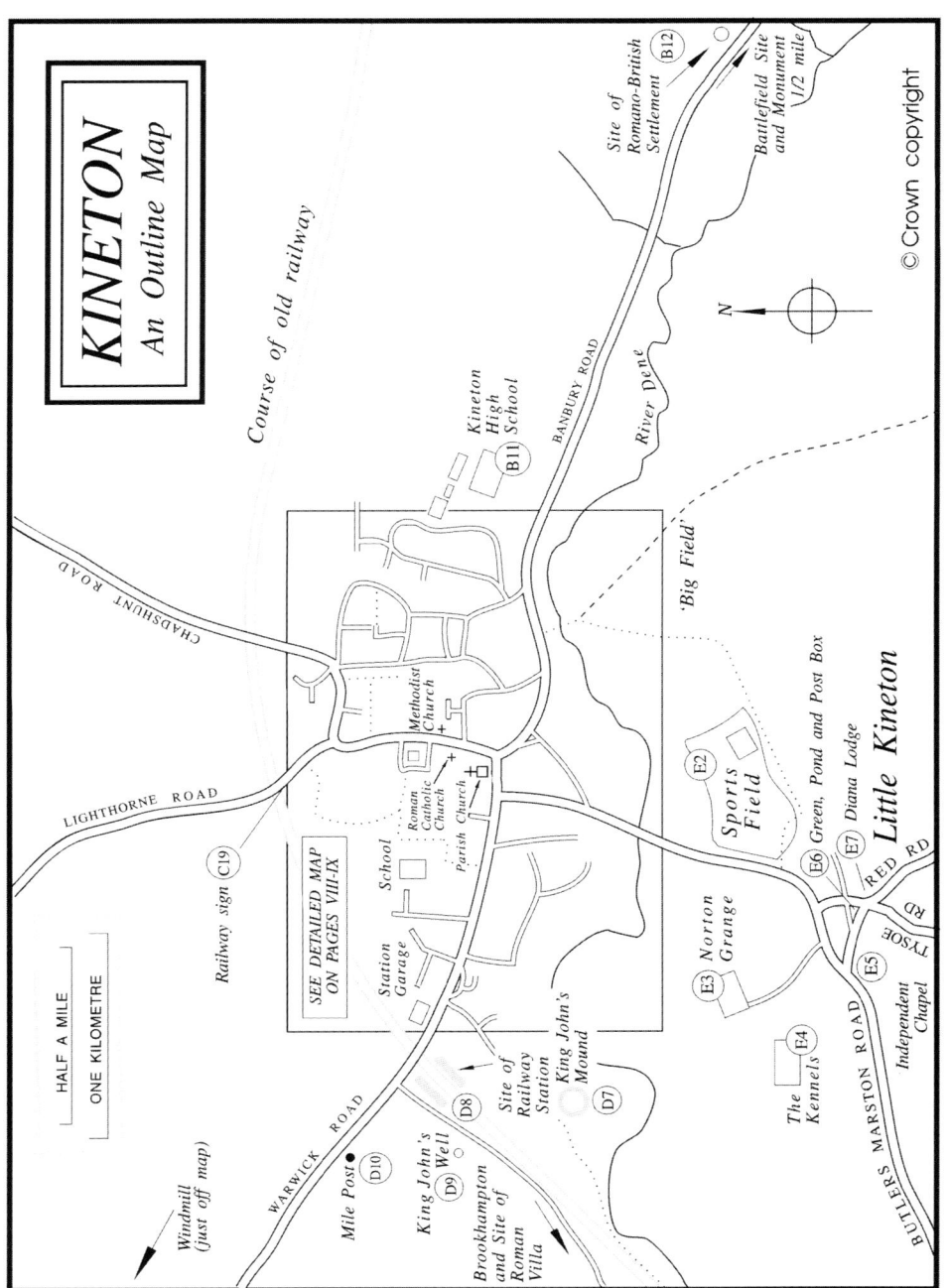

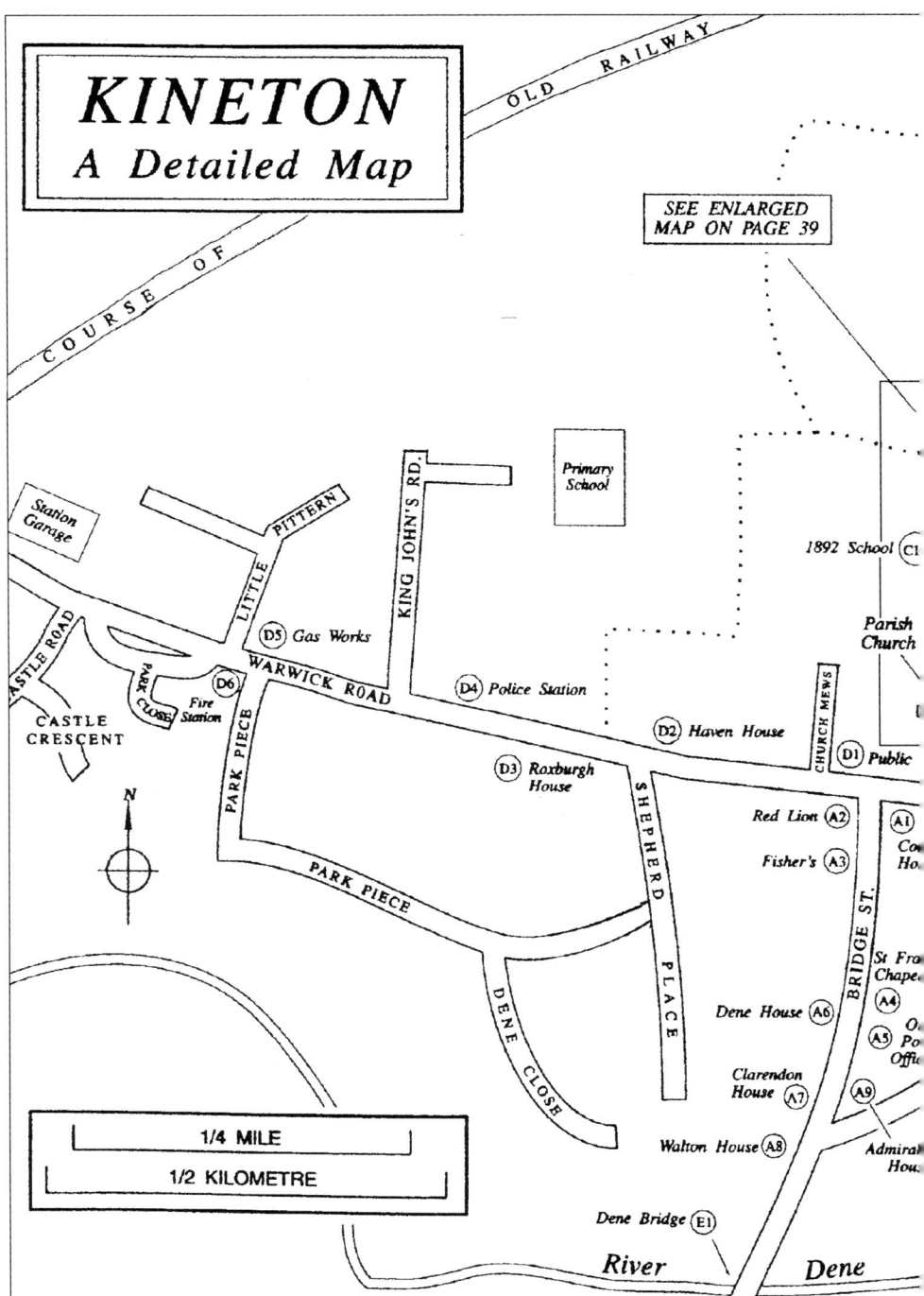

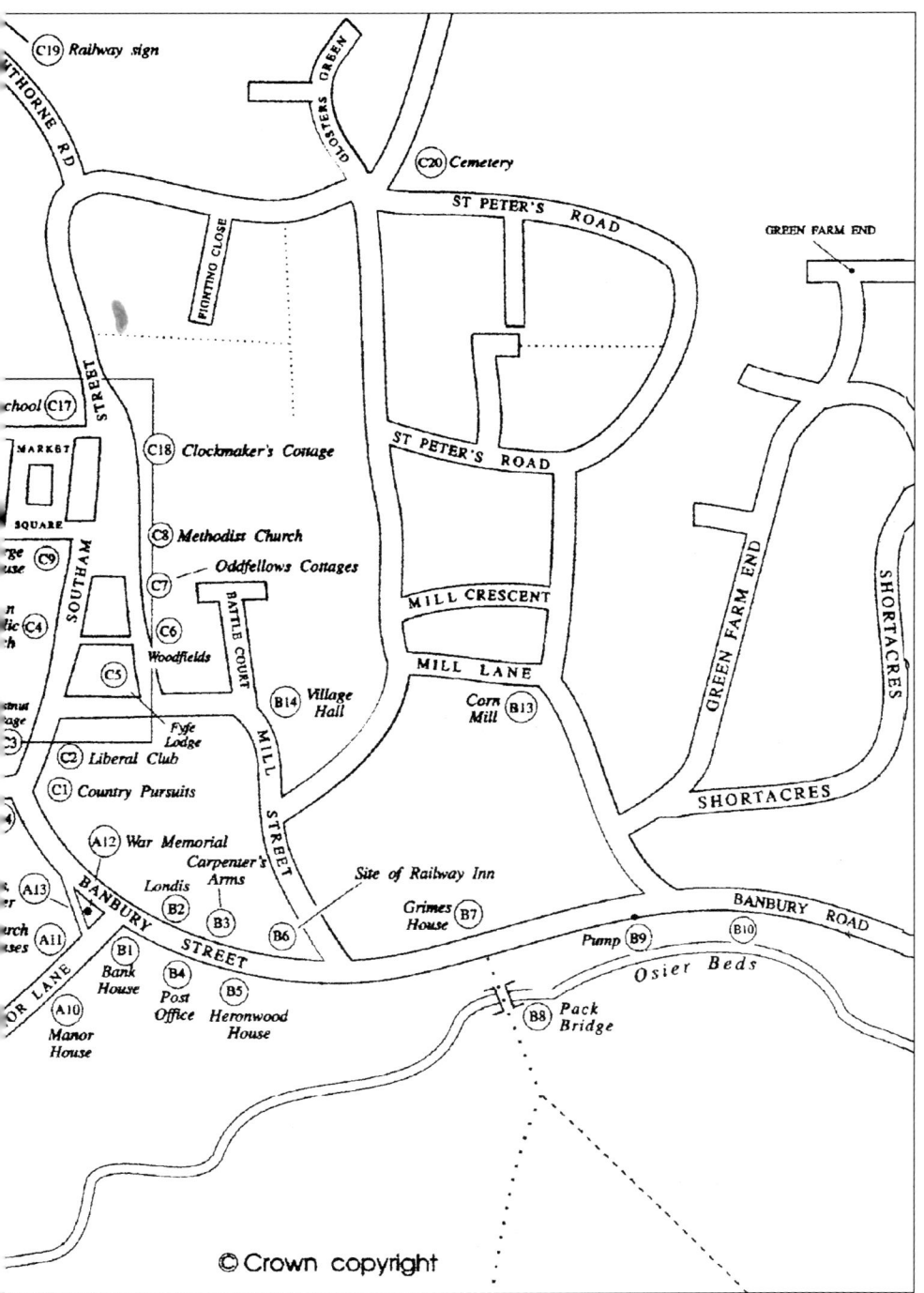

Kineton: The Village and its History

100 years of change in the Warwick Road

CHAPTER 1

AN INTRODUCTORY HISTORY

The Early Days

The difficulty about describing Kineton's first days is that early man left few traces. Later generations built in stone and brick, but it needs a trained archaeologist to interpret the scant remains of the first tents and wooden huts. It is only speculation that allows us to conjure up the images of roots and skins and berries half remembered from our childhood history lessons and to imagine Kineton's first settlers descending from high tracks and simple fortified camps to the fertile valley below Edgehill.

But there are facts to support such images. In prehistoric times much of south east Warwickshire was covered by a glacier which, when melted, left a fertile valley well supplied with streams. A prehistoric trackway, the Jurassic Way, ran along the top of the Edgehill escarpment on its long route south-westwards from the mouth of the Humber to Salisbury Plain and the southern coast beyond. It seems likely that it was from hill forts along the Cotswold escarpment, like the Iron Age Nadbury Camp, constructed about 500 BC at the top of Edgehill, that the first settlers came down to the clay area to the south of the River Avon. There they began to clear and cultivate the land, which in due course became known as the Feldon - 'field land' - an area distinct from the wooded Arden which lay to the north of the Avon. In the fertile, well-watered Feldon lies Kineton.

It is more certain that, during the Roman era (AD 43 - AD 410), a Romano-British settlement existed just outside Kineton **[B12]** and a substantial Roman villa was built at Brookhampton **[D10]**, which lay only a short distance south of the Roman Fosse Way. The outlines of this villa can be made out on aerial photographs, and Roman coins and pottery have been found nearby. When the Romans departed in about AD 410, various Germanic tribes, originally brought in by the Romans as mercenaries, began to overrun the country and develop their separate kingdoms. In AD 634, the border between the two Saxon kingdoms of Hwicce and South Mercia was agreed. Kineton was in Hwicce ; Chadshunt, Burton Dassett and Radway were in South Mercia. This boundary was maintained by the Christian Church when in AD 680 the Dioceses of Lichfield and Worcester were separated, and even today, some 1300 years later, the divisions form the basis of the inter-parish boundaries.

The first recorded mention of Kineton, spelt Cynton (*Cyn* - King's, *ton* - manor), is in the Saxon Charter of AD 969, which states that King Edgar granted land to a Saxon nobleman,

The Roman Villa, Brookhampton. An aerial photograph reveals the outline of a villa in the field between the road to Brookhampton Farm and the old railway track.

named Aelfwold. Both the place-name and the award clearly indicate that, by then, the area around Kineton was in royal hands. There is further confirmation of this in that most famous register of all land ownership in England, the Domesday Book of 1086, where Kineton appears as one of only nine locations in Warwickshire belonging directly to the King. Its name is given as Quintone, the Latin equivalent of Cynton, and from the details of the holdings, it is possible to infer that Kineton was by then a sizeable settlement of some 500 people.

The Middle Ages (1066 - 1485)

By the time of the Norman and the Plantagenet kings, records had become more detailed, and a picture of Kineton that resembles today's village began to emerge. During the Middle Ages the settlement was referred to in official records variously as Kyneton, Kyngton, or Chipping Kyneton (*Chipping* is an Anglo-Saxon word for market, still familiar today in the names of Chipping Campden and Chipping Norton).

The Church of St Peter and land in neighbouring Little Kineton were given to Kenilworth Priory by Henry I early in the 12th century. By 1315 the priors had not only rebuilt the church on its present site but had also enlarged it.

An Introductory History

The reorganisation of local government by King Henry II in about 1160 resulted in the formation of the Kineton Hundred from four of the original Hundreds shown in the Domesday Book. A Hundred was a Saxon sub-division of a county, and probably called this because originally it represented either 100 households or possibly 100 hides of land, a hide being a measure of land between 60 and 120 acres. As the centre of a Hundred, Kineton gained an important administrative role in South Warwickshire, which declined only slowly as other local government organisations developed in the 19th and 20th centuries. As a consequence of the

The 13th century west doorway of St Peter's Church.

feudal system in force throughout medieval times, a royal manor could be given by its owner, the King, as a reward to one of his subjects, and in 1216 King John gave his manor of Kineton Magna to Stephen de Segrave, perhaps as a reward for loyalty during the Baron's Revolt. At about the same time, possibly during King John's troubles with the Barons prior to the signing of the Magna Carta, the Motte and Bailey fortification, known today as King John's Mound [D7] was constructed on the outskirts of the village.

The manor thrived under its new owner, and in 1227, at the request of Stephen de Segrave, Kineton was granted a Market Charter and, two years later, a Charter for Fairs. The Market was held on each Tuesday throughout the year, and was part of a sequence of markets in the area that allowed an opportunity for trade every day - Brailes on Monday, Kineton on Tuesday,

Kineton: The Village and its History

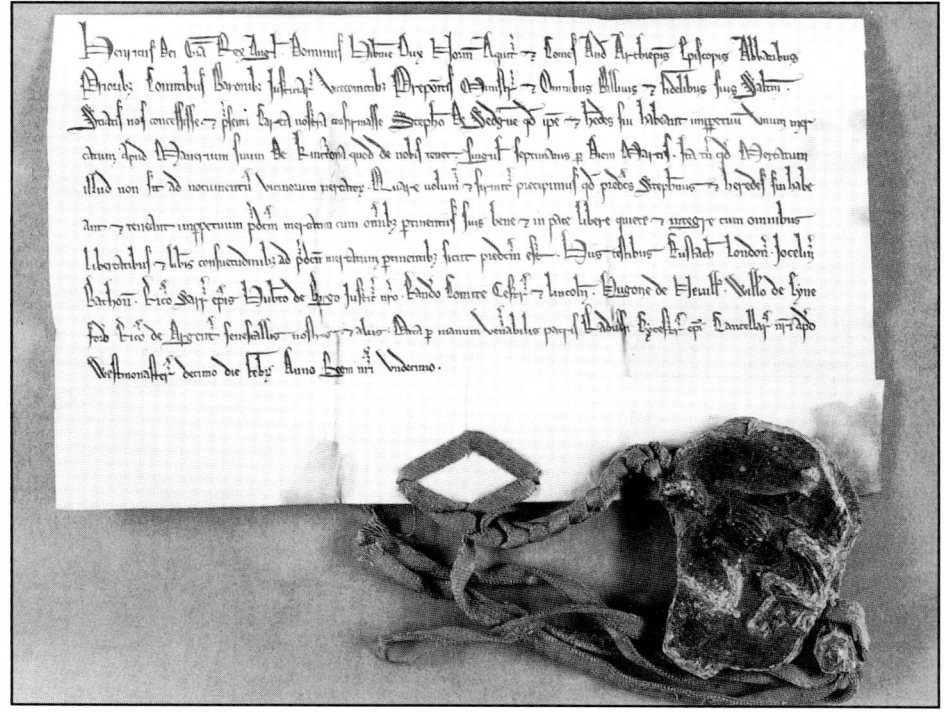

The Market Charter, 1227.

Tysoe on Wednesday, Stratford on Thursday, Burton Dassett on Friday, and Shipston-on-Stour on Saturday. Interestingly, by the 17th century, some markets had failed to thrive and Kineton, Shipston and Southam were the only three survivors in the Feldon.

Although records exist which show that neighbouring Brookhampton became largely depopulated at the time of the Black Death in the middle of the 14th century, those for Kineton have not survived. As far as is known, the actions of Thomas Mowbray, Duke of Norfolk, who was Lord of the Manor of Kineton at about that time, had little effect on Kineton either. In fact and fiction it is well documented that he quarrelled with Bolingbroke (later the Lancastrian King Henry IV) and died in exile in 1399. Even its proximity to powerful Warwick did nothing to disturb Kineton's peaceful slumber through the troubled times which culminated in the Wars of the Roses.

The Tudors and Early Stuarts (1485-1650)

The decisive defeat of Richard III at the Battle of Bosworth in 1485 led to the establishment of firm central government, and this must have had at least some small effect on the village's prosperity. In 1542 the patronage of Kineton Parish Church and its lands were sold off by the Crown, just three years after the Dissolution of the Monasteries by Henry VIII in 1539. They were bought by Robert Burgoyne of Wroxall, who had himself taken an active part in closing down and despoiling the monasteries. The manor remained in the Burgoyne family for the next hundred years.

The Civil War

When civil war broke out in 1642, the geographic position of Kineton suddenly became significant. The village had the misfortune to lie between the opposing forces - between King Charles moving down from Shrewsbury, to march on London, and the Parliamentary Army under the Earl of Essex returning from Gloucester towards Banbury.

The first major clash between Royalist and Parliamentary forces therefore took place in the fields just outside Kineton on 23 October, 1642. For a few days, English history had Kineton centre-stage. Now known as the Battle of Edgehill, this engagement occurred between the King's army of about 12,000 men and a slightly larger Parliamentary force. On the night of 22 October, Parliamentary units were billeted in Kineton and surrounding villages, while the Royalists were in other villages further east. Neither side was aware of the other's presence. Prince Rupert, commanding the Royalist cavalry, was staying in Wormleighton, home of the Spencer family before they moved to Althorp, when some of his scouts surprised and captured a detachment of Essex's troops and so learnt the true situation. The King decided to do battle. Next day his forces were drawn up on the top of Edgehill and Parliamentary troops deployed in the fields between Kineton and Radway, an area now covered by Ministry of Defence ammunition bunkers and closed to the public.

As the Earl of Essex wisely decided to stand his ground rather than attack up a steep slope, the King moved down from the hill in the early afternoon and drew up in front of Radway. Battle was joined. Prince Rupert, the King's hot-headed nephew, led a ferocious cavalry charge against the left flank of Essex's army approximately along the line of the present Banbury-Kineton road, breaking through and entering Kineton, where the Parliamentary baggage train was located. This could well have decisively swung the battle in the King's favour, but so much time was spent in undisciplined looting that the main royalist forces, left without adequate cavalry support, were counter-attacked by Essex and forced back towards Radway. Prince Rupert finally returned and the position was stabilised. By then the light was fading fast and the fighting died down. Both sides remained on the battlefield through a cold, frosty night, with the dead and dying amongst them. Next day the Parliamentary forces began to withdraw north towards their stronghold of Warwick, whilst the King later moved southwards to capture Banbury before proceeding to Oxford. At the time the battle was hailed by the Royalists as a great victory as they had been left in possession of the field of battle, but in reality it was little more than a draw.

It is estimated that about 1,500 men were killed and legend has it that they were buried on the battlefield in the area now known as Grave Ground Coppice. England, and Kineton in particular, had long ceased to be accustomed to carnage on this scale and within a few months two pamphlets had been published in London giving accounts of supernatural happenings in Kineton and the surrounding countryside, including Grave Ground Coppice. People claimed to have seen ghosts in the streets of Kineton and to have heard the cries of dying soldiers.

Kineton: The Village and its History

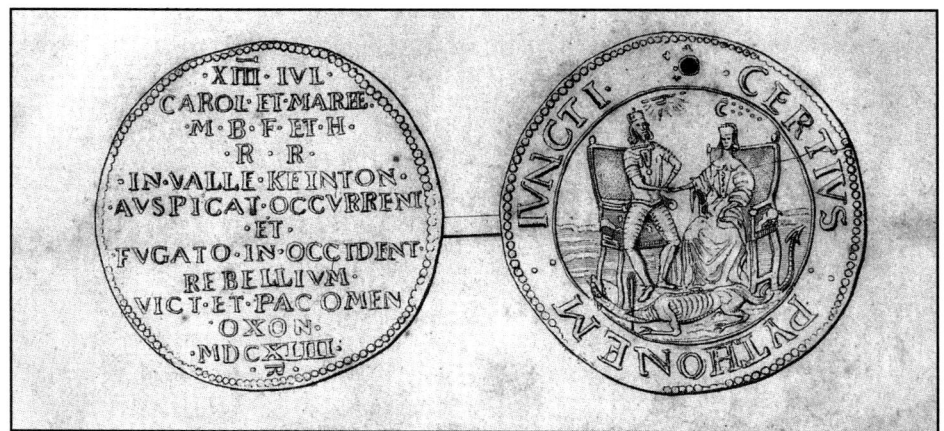

The Kineton Medal struck to commemorate the meeting of King Charles and his Queen in the fields outside Kineton a year after the Battle of Edgehill.

Colonel Lewis Kirke and a party of gentlemen were sent from Oxford by the King to investigate and they too saw the apparitions.

King Charles himself could not have been unduly worried by these stories for he paid a second visit to Kineton less than a year after the battle, when he set up camp to welcome back his wife, Queen Henrietta Maria, on her return from the Continent. She came at the head of a large army bringing supplies for the king. To commemorate this grand occasion and the victory at Roundway Down, near Bath, on the same day, the Kineton Medal was struck. It shows the King and Queen, holding the symbols of Apollo and Diana, side by side within an inscription saying "When united they will more certainly destroy the dragon". The only known surviving specimen is held in the British Museum.

Edgehill was the largest and best known battle in the area, but south Warwickshire was criss-crossed by the opposing armies throughout the remaining three years of the Civil War. Several other battles and skirmishes took place near Kineton and, although there is no obvious evidence in the village itself, nearby Chadshunt church still shows on its walls damage caused by the Royalist cavalry who attacked a detachment of Roundheads seeking sanctuary there.

A Period of Change (1650 - 1850)

After the upheavals of the Civil War, Kineton settled back to a largely uneventful existence for some decades. Few matters occurred that were of real significance to anyone outside the village, but building methods began to produce the lasting architecture that we see around us today.

In the 17th century, Charles Bentley, a supporter of the Parliamentary forces during the Civil War, purchased first the patronage of the Parish Church in 1623, and later the lands that had once belonged to Kenilworth Priory, and the lordship of Little Kineton, where he built a fine manor house. So began the Bentley family's 150-year long involvement with the village

An Introductory History

and the parish church. It was under their patronage during the late 1750s, that Sanderson Miller, of Radway Grange at the foot of Edgehill, was engaged to make the first major alterations to the Parish Church since the 14th century. He enlarged and "improved" the church in the 'Gothick' style for which he was famous. The Bentley family endowed a charity to apprentice poor children, and were the first Lords of the Manor to leave their fine memorials in the parish church.

Some of our earliest knowledge of the arrangement of the village comes from the 1774 Survey of Kineton Magna produced by the Agent to the Earl of Warwick, who was the Lord of the Manor of Great Kineton. Largely from that one source we can begin to envisage the community that was developing in Kineton - who lived in which house, the name and occupation of the head of household, and various other details - all some years before the first official censuses of the population. It indicates an estimated population of between 600 and 650, of whom a third were directly employed in farming or ancillary trades, over a quarter were shopkeepers, and fewer than 50 were in a skilled trade or profession. We can conclude, therefore,

Ridge and furrow in fields near Kineton

that Kineton was a small but thriving market town, heavily dependent on agriculture and on its market, with a wide selection of tradesmen to support both itself and the surrounding villages.

Before the mid-1700s farming methods had changed very little over many centuries. Farm work was largely communal in the standard sized strips of the two or three 'Common Fields'. Even today it is still possible to see the 'ridges and furrows' left by such methods, especially in the flat grassland to the south of the village. Agriculture was mixed, with crops and animals being raised to feed and clothe the family, and with surplus produce being sold in the local markets. From the 14th century, some greedy landowners tried, often illegally, to take over these communal lands for grazing, but during the middle of the 18th century the process of enclosure became more organised. When there was dissent over ownership of land in the open-fields, Parliament appointed Commissioners to consider claims, and as a result of their findings, an 'Enclosure Award' would be made. One such Award was made for Little Kineton in 1733 and another for Kineton in 1792. These Awards allocated to certain individuals areas of land, much of which had previously been part of the Common Fields, and allowed them to be enclosed by hedges and ditches. They also defined public roads, private roads, bridleways and footpaths, thereby providing the legal basis for many present-day rights-of-way. The Awards had a profound effect on farming communities. Predictably, the main beneficiaries tended to be the Lords of the Manor and the wealthier farmers. The smallholders, who had previously scraped a living by cultivating only a furlong or so in the Common Fields, were rarely able to benefit as they could not afford the considerable cost of enclosing their allocated areas. In many cases therefore, these now landless villagers sought employment from more prosperous farmers or moved away in search of places where they could carry on their old way of life. Others found work in the growing urban areas. Many of the field names shown in the Enclosure Awards are still remembered in the locality, and are in use today as house names like 'Flaxlands' and as street names like 'Shortacres', 'Park Piece' and 'Glosters Green'.

Contact with the outside world grew as travel in the countryside became easier. For many centuries, villages had been responsible for the upkeep of their roads and tracks, but with the limited resources at their disposal the results were rarely satisfactory. The heavy clay land of the Feldon meant that for many months of the year the roads and tracks were thick with mud. During the 17th century increasing numbers of wheeled vehicles, including stage coaches attempting much faster journeys, resulted in further deterioration. Consequently, from the beginning of the 18th century, Turnpike Acts were passed in Parliament to enable local Trusts to be set up to improve and maintain specific routes financed by tolls charged to all travellers. The name Turnpike came from the movable barrier used at the tollhouses to prevent travellers passing through until they had paid their dues. By the beginning of the 19th century road conditions had been much improved.

The first turnpike to affect Kineton was a section from Wellesbourne to Upton at the top of Edgehill which was started in 1770, thus completing a route from Birmingham to London via Stratford. An old milepost still standing on Pittern Hill **[D12]** possibly dates from this time. Much later, in 1852, as part of one of the last Turnpike Acts to be passed, a turnpike connected Kineton to Southam, and provided access to the main line railway at Harbury Station. The tollhouses that served this route, both at Kineton and Gaydon, remain today as private dwellings, one exactly on the parish boundary at the appropriately named 'Half Mile Cottage' on the Chadshunt Road. For a period during the 18th and the first part of the 19th century, stage coaches ran through Kineton on their journey between Stratford or Kidderminster and London, some stopping at the Red Lion whilst others may have used the Swan.

These improvements to road communications sounded the death knell for Kineton's market. Traders were now able to travel greater distances to the larger markets of Warwick and Stratford and eventually, in 1840, Kineton market closed. The old Market House was pulled down and a Church of England School built in its place in the middle of the square **[C12]**.

During the 19th century the monopoly of the Church of England in Kineton was broken when non-conformist groups began to establish their own places of worship. In 1813 a group of dissenters moved from Ettington and started to meet regularly in Little Kineton, and in 1842 the first Wesleyan Methodist Chapel was built in Southam Street.

Victorian and Edwardian Expansion

In 1863, an enterprising group of local tradesmen formed the Kineton Gas Light, Coal and Coke Company, which initially supplied the village, and later Compton Verney and Combroke, with gas from its works on the Warwick Road. Among the buildings eventually lit by gas was the parish church, which had been altered and enlarged once again to cater for the large numbers that attended church on Sundays. Records show that in 1851 about 300 attended morning service at the parish church, and 400 went to the afternoon service. At the same time the Methodists numbered about 70 in the morning and 90 in the afternoon, and the Independents expected about 55 at their afternoon service. The Methodist chapel was much enlarged in 1893, when it was rebuilt as we see it today. The Independent chapel closed at about the turn of the century.

By the mid-19th century railway lines were being constructed all over Britain, finally bringing the era of the stage coach to an end. Kineton was not on any of the early railway routes linking the large cities, though it was eventually included in one of the many branch lines that later linked the major lines. By the end of 1871 it was easy to take a train to London by changing at Fenny Compton, and only two years later, in 1873, the branch line had been extended to connect the London and North Western line at Blisworth to the Great Western line at Stratford, with up to 10 trains a day through Kineton Station. The line running through Kineton, at first called the East and West Junction Railway, and later, after amalgamation, the Stratford-upon-Avon and Midland Junction Railway, was used not only by passengers but also by goods and cattle traffic, and by the increasingly active Warwickshire Hunt.

The emergence of the Warwickshire Hunt as one of the foremost packs in the country dominated life in Kineton in the period up to the first World War, and beyond. The lordships of the manors of both Kineton and Little Kineton had been acquired by the Lords Willoughby de Broke, all keen hunting men. In 1839 it was decided that Hunt kennels should be constructed in Little Kineton. They were among the first purpose-built kennels in the country. The solid base of the Hunt in Kineton attracted many people to the village, and increasingly they bought or hired houses in the area for the hunting season. The needs of the

Kineton: The Village and its History

Hunt, and of those who came for the hunting season, provided a source of considerable employment in the village and gave a stimulus to local trade.

For many hundreds of years the village had been called Kineton or Kington indiscriminately, but at last, by the end of the 19th century, the name Kington fell entirely into disuse, and it was clearly 'Kineton'. Its population had grown to 1000, just doubling its size in the thousand years since the Domesday Book.

The Modern Age (1914 - Present Day)
The First World War

Instability in Europe finally erupted into full scale conflict when Britain declared war on Germany on 4 August, 1914. Life in Kineton changed almost overnight. Newspapers reported that no fewer than 110 horses from the Kineton area were commandeered by the Army in the very first month of the war. Not surprisingly, stable lads and kennelmen of the Warwickshire Hunt were among the first to sign up for "King and Country". In the almost feudal atmosphere

The War Memorial unveiled in 1921

of a village devoted to serving the wealthier sections of society, a very high regard was paid to patriotism and service to one's country, and there is little doubt that the village gentry encouraged their employees to enlist. By the end of the war over 250 men from Kineton (practically the whole of the working population) had joined the services, and at the same time some 200 women were 'in uniform' at Kineton's Voluntary Aid Hospital. The hospital was one of the first five wartime hospitals to be formed in Warwickshire, opening in November 1914. By early 1917 it had 100 beds in three Kineton properties, one of which was Kineton House. This is now the Mansion House, Norton Grange, but was then the home of Joshua Fielden, whose wife was one of the Commandants of the hospital. The hospital finally closed in December 1918 after having treated no less than 2,168 wounded, with only one fatality. Much was made of the need to entertain the wounded soldiers, and almost the whole of the village must have been involved in one way or another in running and financing this fine institution. In addition, Kineton played host to Belgian refugees, knitted garments for the troops, billeted and entertained a Territorial Army Royal Engineer Company for a few weeks, and formed its own Home Defence Volunteer unit.

The War Memorial, paid for by public subscriptions, was unveiled in 1921 and bears the names of 38 Kineton men known to have been killed in the war.

Between the Wars

Once the war was over and the men had returned to the village, an attempt was made to rebuild shattered lives. Despite a severe economic depression, the village started to expand, with the building of the first council houses in King John's Road on land previously known as Paradise Close. The Warwickshire Hunt overcame its wartime difficulties and provided a full social life for its members, and the village again started to prosper by giving service to the wealthy visitors. The first cars which had been laid up during the war years appeared once more on the streets, and car ownership increased rapidly. In 1924 the Kineton Green Bus Service was established, but soon after a disastrous fire at their bus depot in 1934 the company was taken over by the Stratford Blue Bus Company. Despite the competition from railway and buses, a carrier, George Styles, was still operating in Kineton in 1936 using a small lorry with an open back, thus maintaining the stout tradition of the 19th century carriers who had served the village so well. Electricity arrived in the village in the 1920s, and within five years of the construction in 1927 of the sub-station in Banbury Street, electric street lights were replacing the old gas lamps.

The Second World War

From the outset Kineton, in its countryside setting, took evacuee children. Their numbers were swelled by the homeless, particularly from Coventry after the devastating bombing of the city on the night of 14 November 1940. The village sent its young men into the Services again, and formed a Local Defence Volunteer Detachment, initially armed with only the most primitive of weapons. The 'Home Guard' manned look-out posts to watch for enemy aircraft and any airmen who might have bailed out, and on one occasion they captured some of the aircrew from a crashed German bomber. A Territorial Army Searchlight detachment was deployed just outside Little Kineton, and a number of Czech troops who had escaped to Britain were billeted in the village in what is now Haven House. They formed part of one of the machine-gun companies of a brigade based in the Leamington area. Some of their training was carried out at Compton Verney, which for a time housed a camouflage unit of the Royal Engineers developing the Haslor smoke machine in its smoke school. A number of these Czech soldiers married local girls and settled in the area after the war.

The war forced every farmer to make radical changes. As in the rest of the country, the County War Agricultural Committee dictated that as much grassland as possible be put into

War work in the Lucas factory. Kineton, 1943

arable and root crops, and as a result nearly all the grassland in Kineton was ploughed up. Members of the Women's Land Army, or Land Girls as they were better known, were drafted in to take the place of the men away in the Services, and they worked on many of the local farms.

Early in the war, some light industrial manufacturing industry, making bomb relays and sights for the Lucas company, was established in Kineton and staffed by local women, first in the outhouses of the Swan Inn before moving to the telephone exchange on Brookhampton Lane. Later, during the build-up to D Day, a temporary army camp was set up on Park Piece - then still an open field. The Women's Institute Hall was used as a canteen for the troops. A Red Cross Hospital and Recuperation Centre was opened at Kineton House, staffed locally as it had been in the First World War, although this time acting as a civilian hospital for general nursing cases and for home casualties.

And so, after nearly six weary years, the Second World War finally came to an end with the surrender of the Japanese on 15 August, 1945. During this time ten men from Kineton lost their lives in the fighting, and in 1947 their names were added to the War Memorial that had been erected little more than twenty-five years before.

The Modern Village

The effects of the war brought many lasting changes to the village. Perhaps the greatest of these dates back to 1941 when a large ammunition depot was established just outside Kineton. This still occupies many acres of farmland and has obliterated several Kineton farms - Battle Farm and Thistleton Farm among them - and it has put many miles of public footpaths and bridleways and almost all of the site of the Battle of Edgehill behind wire. This depot, the largest of its kind in Britain and probably in Europe, is likely to remain here well into the 21st century. Later, the re-opening on 1 March 1954 of the wartime Gaydon airfield as a V-bomber base generated useful employment for the area, but also, less desirably, unforgettable levels of

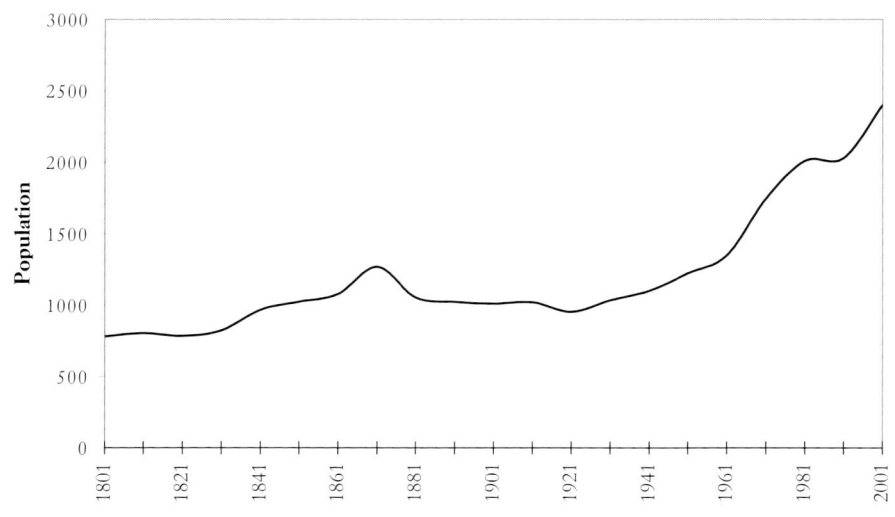

Kineton Population Growth.
The peak in 1871 reflects the presence of navvies building the railway.

noise. Happily it closed in 1980 and is now used as a research centre and test track by the Rover Group. The great bomb-storage bunkers which remain as a chilling reminder of the area's vulnerability during the airfield's active period are now used for the National Film Institute archives.

Kineton: The Village and its History

The steady increase in the ownership of motor vehicles and the construction of better roads and motorways has led to the shrinking of the rail network. Kineton Station closed for passengers in 1952 and to goods traffic a few years later. The improvements in the road network have also allowed people to travel considerable distances to work and many have moved out of towns into rural areas like Kineton. In 1951, the population was only 1,223, but by 1971 this figure had risen sharply to 1,745, an increase reflected in the construction of houses in St Peter's Road, Castle Road and the completion of others in Park Piece and Dene Close. Growth continued in the 1970s and 80s with the developments of Green Farm End, Shortacres, Fighting Close and Norton Grange, and the population had topped 2,000 by 1991. The further completion in the 1990s of Glosters Green, Little Pittern and other smaller developments in Kineton and Little Kineton indicates that by the turn of the century a population approaching 2,500 is very likely. Once again the population will have doubled - but this time in only 50 years.

Kineton can no longer be considered a market town or even an agricultural village, but has become, like so many of its neighbours, more of a dormitory settlement in rural surroundings, where few of its residents work on the land or even in the village itself, and where an increasing number are retired.

Kineton at the Millennium - The Way Forward

This is perhaps a good time to reflect on the past two thousand years of Kineton's history, to understand how and why the village has developed in the way that it has, and perhaps also, to applaud the work, dedication and foresight of some of the past leaders of the community. What does the future hold for Kineton? No one can tell for certain, but it seems likely that current trends will continue at least for some years. Despite the small number of people involved, agriculture will surely continue to play a crucial part in moulding the surrounding countryside. Pressure to build more houses for a fragmenting and longer-living society will certainly remain but will have to be carefully controlled if the village is to retain its character and not overload its limited facilities. With the opening by the Peter Moores Foundation of a major Art Gallery at Compton Verney, with the improvements at King John's Castle and the Dene Valley, and with the possible siting of an Edgehill Battle Museum on the outskirts of the village, the future of Kineton seems assured.

Chapter 2

For the Visitor - The Parish Church and Five Walks Round Kineton

The five historical walks through Kineton suggested here all start from the churchyard gate on the Warwick Road. Two lie straight ahead, down Bridge Street, two lie to the left, and one to the right. The information given during the walks is only brief, but many aspects are covered in greater depth in Chapters 3 and 4. Before setting off it is well worth spending some time in the Parish Church, which has served as a focal point for life in Kineton for about a thousand years and reflects much of the village's history.

The Parish Church

Although there is no mention of a church in the Saxon charter of AD 969, it is probable that there was a simple wooden structure in the vicinity. There was certainly one in Kineton before 1135, for in that year Henry I gave a church, already dedicated to St Peter, to the Priory of Kenilworth. Some time late in the thirteenth century work began upon a new church, and in July 1315 the completed building, probably consisting only of a nave, chancel and tower, was reconsecrated.

The only survival from this period is the handsome west tower, with its fine doorway and small window above. The pinnacles and battlements around the tower have inevitably been restored many times, but their present form may be similar to the original outline. The stone clock dial on the south wall of the tower was installed a few years before the existing clock, which dates from 1884. The present clock was chosen at a London exhibition by a group of Kineton businessmen, and paid for by public subscription. The wrought-iron weathervane was made by Thomas Coates in 1794. In the Bell Chamber are six fine bells cast by Abraham Rudhall I, four dated 1703, one 1716 and the tenor inscribed "Prosperity to this towne and all our benefactors. AR 1717."

The nave and chancel, although both of the same toffee-coloured stone as the tower, are of much later date. In the late 1750s, the vicar, the Rev William Talbot, engaged Sanderson Miller, the gentleman architect and country squire from nearby Radway Grange, to 'improve' the church in the Gothick manner by enlarging the existing nave with a north aisle and by adding two transepts. It would seem that the cost of the rebuilding was met privately - possibly even by William Talbot himself - as no charge whatsoever was made to the parish of Kineton itself. A series of three-light, ogee-headed windows were introduced at that time. Then, between

Kineton: The Village and its History

St Peter's Church about 1810. Captain James Saunders' drawing shows the building before its Victorian alterations.

the mid 1870s and 1882, following the precedent set by William Talbot, the Rev Francis Miller also carried out an ambitious rebuilding programme, which transformed the church, both inside and out, into something very similar to the present-day building, at a cost of some £4,174.

The 13th century west doorway, which leads into the church through a vaulted passage, appears unusually truncated because the ground level has risen about three feet over the centuries. Inside, above the entrance, is the small West Gallery, all that remains of an L-shaped gallery that ran along the west and north walls and which was reached by a staircase in the north-west corner. Today this corner is home to the 19th century 'naughty boys cage', which came from the village school and which was used by various headteachers during that period as a punishment for bad behaviour and truancy.

Further down the north aisle is an iron-bound, round-topped chest from the sixteenth century, complete with nine hinges and three hasps and padlocks. The chest would have been used for the safe keeping of the parish records and church valuables. The keys to the three locks were kept by three separate people—the parson, and the two churchwardens—a simple security measure which that meant that no-one could gain access without the presence of all three men.

The north aisle also holds a well preserved, recumbent figure of a 14th century priest with clerical tonsure. The flag in the north transept was flown by Admiral Sir Walter Cowan at the surrender of the German Fleet in the Firth of Forth on 21 November 1918, while the flag on the south wall by the brass war memorial flew over the Clarendon House VAD Hospital in Bridge Street during the 1914-1918 War.

The chancel itself was not always in the reasonable state of repair seen today. Traditionally, responsibility for the upkeep of the nave lay with the villagers, while the chancel was maintained by the tithe owners (often the Lord of the Manor). In 1684, diocesan inspections drew attention to "a very bad earthen floor" and to the fact that the graves of Charles Bentley and his daughter Frances were not filled in. In the 1820s the churchwardens complained that it took many hours to wheel away the snow coming through the chancel roof.

One of the Bentley mermaids in the Parish Church.

The church contains several monuments to the families of the later Lords of the Manor, including the Bentley monuments displaying their heraldic mermaid. There are also memorials of some of the vicars of the parish, and of various villagers remembered for their service to the church and to the community. These are described in the church guide *The Parish Church of St Peter*, by Peter Titchmarsh, from which most of this description has been drawn.

Return to the churchyard path through the door at the west end of the church.

Walk A - Bridge Street, Manor Lane and part of Banbury Street

This walk starts from the churchyard gate and proceeds to the bridge at the bottom of Bridge Street, from which point it is possible to return to the church by way of Manor Lane and the top end of Banbury Street or, to extend the walk further, by taking the Little Kineton Walk (Walk E, page 51). Without the extension this is a walk of less than half a mile.

From the churchyard gate cross directly to the top of Bridge Street. On the left hand corner

The Court House [A1] stands on the site of what, in the 18th century, was part of a pig farm with lands running over Manor Lane and down to the river at the bottom of Bridge Street. This may explain why Manor Lane was once called Hog Lane or Swine Street. The present house was built in 1807-8 by Edward Welchman, a surgeon whose memorial in the Parish Church describes him as

> an old resident of this town, who conducted an extensive and laborious practice for upwards of forty years, when being deprived of his sight he relinquished his profession.

Use of part of the building as a surgery continued into the 20th century.

The Court House, Bridge Street

In 1863, the Honourable W H J North, later 11th Lord North, the master of the Warwickshire Hunt, purchased the house and had it fitted up for use during the hunting season. For this reason the building was known for many years as 'North Lodge'. When it was sold in 1873, it was described as

> a capital Hunting Box, comprising 12 bed and dressing rooms, day and night nurseries, spacious entrance hall, drawing, dining, and breakfast rooms, with ample domestic offices, good stabling and coach-house, with groom's room over, small lawn, pleasure grounds, and gardens.

Rather misleadingly, the building became known as 'The Court House' some thirty years before 1950, when the Petty Sessions Court was transferred here from the Women's Institute

Hall in Mill Lane. The court was finally closed in 1992 and was replaced by the public library, which moved here from the Market Square.

Opposite, on the right hand corner

Red Lion House [A2], now private accommodation, was formerly the Red Lion Inn. It used to have a date-stone with the year 1677 inscribed on it, and in 1690, "at the house of William Ricketts, being the sign of the Red Lion", the inhabitants of Whatcote were presented before the justices for failing to maintain the road to Kineton. For much of the 19th century the Petty Sessions court was held alternately at the Red Lion and at the nearby Swan Inn [A14]. The Red Lion has also served as the meeting place for organisations as diverse as the Literary Society, the Provident Friendly Society, and the Quoits Club, as well as the dressing room for the Kineton United Football Club in the 1960s. In the early years of the 20th century it was also the home of the intriguingly titled Sparrow and Rat Club, which aimed to rid the surrounding farms of 'vermin', understandably rats, but also sparrows. In the first year of the Club's existence nearly 3,500 sparrows and 2,500 rats were killed by its members. In the late 1820s the *Britannia* stagecoach would call here on three mornings a week at 10.30am, on its way between Kidderminster and London, returning the following afternoon at 4pm. After the closure of the Market House in 1840, the yard at the rear was used for regular livestock sales, and the local schoolmaster would often note in the school log-book "several boys absent this afternoon, it being Kineton Monthly Stock Sale".

Just below Red Lion House are the premises of

Fisher's [A3], which have been in the hands of the Fisher family since 1888, when Joseph Fisher, a draper with a shop in Stratford, opened another in Kineton. For a time the shop combined china dealing with the drapery business but in recent years has been a hairdresser's. An obituary for Joseph Fisher, who died in 1926, records that

> for 47 years he was a Wesleyan lay preacher. His sermons were picturesque and dramatic, dealing principally with Old Testament subjects, and were easy to remember. He was much in demand for anniversaries and harvest festivals.

Much earlier, when part of the present site was offered for sale in 1819, the property included a brewhouse, a comb shop converted into a bakehouse, and "a half part of the pump".

Further down on the opposite side of the road is

St Francis Chapel [A4]. The building of the first Roman Catholic church in Kineton since the Reformation owed much to the initiative of Mr and Mrs Francis Sumner, who came to live in Dene House on the opposite side of the road in 1916. During the latter part of World War I they had given hospitality to several Belgian refugees, and had arranged for a Mass to be provided for them in their home. After the war, arrangements were made with the priest in Avon Dassett for Mass to be said regularly - first once a month, then every Sunday - in the dining-room of Dene House, and these services were attended by "the scattered and isolated Catholics of Kineton and the villages round about."

By 1922 a church was needed in Kineton, and the Sumners were part of an influential committee that accomplished this in 1927 by acquiring a building that had recently served as a pump maker's workshop. In transforming what contemporary reports described as "an old tumble-down Tudor barn" into a church the architect kept many of its ancient features - the old tiles and characteristic string course outside and the original oak beams and rafters inside. A beam from the demolished Priory at Warwick was added above the altar, and the church dedicated to St Francis of Assisi.

For over forty years the church was served from Avon Dassett, but could hold only 68 people. When in 1971 Kineton was made the new centre of the parish, a presbytery was acquired in Market Square. More room was needed, and a new church **[C4]** was built in Southam Street. The Bridge Street building became a private dwelling.

Further down this side

The Old Post Office [A5] still has its title above the lower door. In 1885 William H Wilkins, tailor and woollen draper, was appointed Postmaster of Kineton in succession to Thomas Garrett. It would seem that he was happier than his predecessor with the conditions of employment, for Thomas Garrett resigned after thirty years as postmaster with the comment that "the remuneration is not in proportion to the onerous and extra duties to be discharged". Thus on 11 January 1885 the telegraphic apparatus, letter box, and other fittings were removed

Outside the Post Office in Bridge Street

to the new office from the old one at the top of Banbury Street, and the new postmaster settled in. In 1892 Mrs Wilkins succeeded her late husband "ably assisted by several members of her family, who have already in so many ways given ample proof of their efficiency". The association of the Wilkins family with the Post Office continued until 1942, when Mrs Bella Worrall took over as postmistress. The building ceased to be the Post Office in 1969, and for a short period housed a betting shop.

On the opposite side of Bridge Street is

Dene House [A6], for which there is a reference in 1759 to "a messuage, brewhouse, edifices, barns, stables, yards, orchards, gardens and backsides in the possession of Elizabeth Hewet, widow". By 1854, the copyhold had been sold to John Griffin, who continued in business as a grocer and wine and spirit merchant for sixty-seven years, as well being churchwarden for fifty-three years and "the mainstay of Kineton in all parochial affairs". Soon after John Griffin's

John Griffin's grocery shop in Bridge Street.

death in 1915, the property was sold to the prominent Roman Catholic, Francis G Sumner, JP, who was to be so active in the establishment of the chapel across the street. In the 1930s the outbuildings were the Ministry of Labour Employment Exchange, and in 1947 housed the Roundwood Press, Gordon Norwood's noted printing and publishing firm responsible for many books of local historical interest. During the Second World War Dene House was occupied by Dr Clement J Wells who, having joined the Royal Army Medical Corps, was present when the German Nazi leader Heinrich Himmler committed suicide in 1945.

A little lower down the road is

Clarendon House [A7], standing on land previously occupied by two houses which were destroyed by fire in the middle of the 18th century. Since then it has had a varied history as private residence, boarding house, military hospital and, twice, as an educational establishment.

Clarendon House Ladies' School was opened here by Miss Webb in 1884, and continued until 1905. It provided both day and boarding education for girls from middle class homes in such subjects as English grammar and analysis, French, drawing, music, scripture and English history. The young ladies also produced "paintings and drawings of very great variety displaying taste, care, and talent", as well as "plain and fancy needlework, executed in an artistic manner". Miss Webb's younger brother, Guernsey Walsingham Webb, ran a school for young gentlemen in the same building until he was appointed principal of the more prestigious Middle School **[D3]** on the Warwick Road. During the First World War Clarendon House was used as a military hospital, and although in 1914 it started with only 20 beds, the establishment had before long expanded to include neighbouring Walton House **[A8]** and Kineton House **[E3]** in Little Kineton. Its remarkable record was marred by the death of only one casualty ; ironically this unfortunate soldier fell through a trapdoor while preparing for a concert just after Armistice Day.

Clarendon House VAD hospital with Walton House beyond.

After the Second World War "good cooking and a real welcome" was offered at the Clarendon Guest House. Then, in 1954, the Manor Lane School transferred to the premises for a period. It is now a private residence.

Next door

Walton House [A8] was previously Walton Farmhouse. At different times it has served as the farmhouse for a number of farms. The building on the site in 1774 was rebuilt a few years later by Henry Stiles, a baker. During the 19th century the 16th Lord Willoughby de Broke made it the farmhouse for Castle Farm, which was on land mainly to the east of Kineton. In due course it became the farmhouse for Walton Farm, and eventually a private residence when the accommodation for Walton Farm moved to a new building on the Banbury Road. During the First World War it was part of the Clarendon House VAD Hospital. More recently it was the home of the Honourable Mrs Patience Hanbury (1873-1965). Sister of the 19th Lord Willoughby de Broke, she is well remembered for the active role she played in many village organisations, including the Women's Institute, the District Nursing Association, the Cricket Club and many forms of amateur drama.

Across the road, on the corner with Manor Lane is

The Admiral's House [A9], named after Admiral Sir Walter (Titch) Cowan, Bart., KCB, MVO, DSO, who lived here for more than twenty-five years until his death in 1956. Born in 1871, he entered the Navy in 1884, and, like young Winston Churchill, fought at the Battle of Omdurman, for which he was awarded the DSO. He then took part in the Boer War and World War I. Amazingly, he then served throughout the Second World War, having somehow contrived to join the Commandos at the age of 70. For his great gallantry he was awarded a bar to the DSO that he had won so many years before. He is buried in Kineton cemetery **[C22]** and the flag flown by his ship at the surrender of the German Fleet in 1918 hangs in the Parish Church.

Amongst earlier residents of the house, the history of which can be traced back to the early 1700s, were Thomas and Elizabeth Court. Thomas Court, plumber and glazier, died in 1871, but his widow continued the business from the house, advertising herself as "sanitary plumber, paper hanger and glazier, newsagent and stationer".

From here it is possible to return to the centre of the village by turning left along Manor Lane or to carry straight on towards Little Kineton (see Walk E, page 51) about half a mile away.

Turning left, at the far end of Manor Lane, set behind the brick wall and modern extensions on the right, stands

The Manor House [A10], now a residential nursing home, though originally the Manor House for Kineton Magna. It was seldom occupied by a Lord of the Manor, but often served as the home of his steward or land agent. Francis Aylworth was living at the Manor House even before he purchased the Lordship from Lord Berkeley in 1575. Residents of the present building have included the Rev William Talbot, vicar of Kineton, and Hugh Williams, architect of the Hunt Kennels in Little Kineton. Then, with the growth of the Hunt, a succession of wealthy families used it as their 'hunting box' or 'lodge' for the season. In 1899 the Parish Magazine suggested

> it will be of interest to our readers to know that the new Bishop of Bangor, the Right Rev Watkin Herbert Williams, formerly Dean of St Asaph, is a native of Kineton, having been born at the Manor House.

During the late 1970s, while the Manor House was being run as a hotel, the owner bred Caspian horses, a miniature breed originating in Iran.

The stone cottages on the opposite side of the road are known as

The Church Houses [A11]. Until 1999 some were still owned by the parish church. They are a reminder of the provision made by the parish in the 19th century to meet its obligation to the poor and needy; other houses owned by the parish for this purpose are now gone. A register of 1821 records a number of seats in the church allocated to "houses occupied by Parish Paupers - top of Hog Lane". Later, while reminiscing about Kineton in the 1870s, William Rawlins recalled that the roofs of these cottages were thatched and that across the gable-end there was a board about six feet long and nine inches high bearing the inscription 'Church Houses' in large letters. The plot of land on which the cottages stand appears to have been part of the Rectorial Tithes of Kenilworth Priory, and may have been given to the Priors by King Henry I when he gave St Peter's Church and other land in Little Kineton. The houses were not listed in the 1774 survey for the Lord of the Manor, a further indication that they did not then belong to him. In 1850, the plot contained ten cottages, but some have since been pulled down and others joined together.

Turn left to

The War Memorial [A12], which bears the names of the 38 Kineton men who died in the First World War 1914-1918, and the ten names of those killed during the Second World War 1939-1945. At the end of the First World War the Green at the centre of the village was chosen as the place for a memorial to men who gave their lives in the service of their country. Designs considered by a specially appointed committee included a soldier bearing a scroll, and drinking troughs for horses and dogs, and suggested materials included bronze and Portland stone. The final choice was a Hornton stone memorial based closely on the medieval cross at Brigstock in Northamptonshire, to be erected by Booth's, the then fashionable stonemasons with quarries on Edge Hill.

The Memorial was unveiled on Sunday 10 July 1921, in the presence of the Bishop of Coventry and General Gage of Farnborough, as well as a large number of the village who had contributed to its cost. At the top are four badges: a Royal Coat of Arms representing the Army, a Naval Crown for the Senior Service, an Antelope for the Warwickshire Yeomanry, and a Bear and Ragged Staff for the Royal Warwickshire Regiment. From the inscriptions it is sadly evident that some families suffered the loss of several sons. Three Askew brothers were killed. Of the five sons of the Fisher family - then Bridge Street drapers - only three returned, for one was killed on the Somme and another died in the Balkans after a brilliant career in the Bulgarian Resistance, for which he was decorated with the Bulgarian 'Soldier's Cross'. The two sons of the Methodist minister, Franklyn Smith, were both killed in France during his three year tour of duty in Kineton - the elder one, fighting alongside his younger brother, received his first Military Cross in the action in which his brother was killed. For more details read *Kineton in the Great War* by Gillian Ashley-Smith.

Beside the War Memorial are the premises of

H C Lewis, Butcher [A13], a family firm which has carried on the butchery business here for more than a century through three generations. Started by Thomas Hooper Lewis in 1888, it was kept up by his widow, Mary. She was succeeded by their son, Harry Cheadle Lewis, under whose name the business is continued by another Thomas. Not only was the shop one of the first five premises to be lit by electricity - a special deal with the Leamington Electrical Company to advertise the new technology - but also it was among the first to have a telephone.

In front of the shop is a three-step mounting block.

The adjoining house was originally built in an orchard by Thomas Hall sometime before 1774. In the early 1850s it became the Post Office run by Thomas Garrett, who somehow managed to combine his work as postmaster with that as a butcher for over 34 years. When he resigned in 1885 the Post Office was transferred to Bridge Street.

At the end of the War Memorial Green,

The Swan Inn [A14], has a carved stone bearing the date 1668 above its entrance on the Warwick Road. In 1682, the Inn was one of the few in Warwickshire to house a 'Visitation' by the Herald's College, which was conducting a survey of arms and family descent in the Midlands. When a new landlord was sought in 1849, it was described as

> an old established and well accustomed Commercial Inn and Excise Office now in full trade and comprising every requisite convenience, with excellent stabling, spacious yard, and walled garden.

It seems likely that it had served as a coaching inn, although no timetable reference has been traced. As mentioned above, the Petty Sessions Court was held alternately at the Swan and at the nearby Red Lion [A2] for much of the 19th century. The Swan, like the Red Lion, also served as the meeting place for many Kineton organisations including, for a time, the Old

The Swan Inn, Banbury Street, before 1905.

Friendly Society (established in 1785), the New Friendly Society, and annual meetings of the Kineton Gas Company, the Kineton and Wellesbourne Turnpike Trust, and the Horticultural Society. During the First World War the licensee claimed to be providing stabling for 30 horses, although when the inn was inspected for billeting purposes in 1917 it was said to be suitable for only 20 horses - but also 50 men!

The skittle alley on the first floor still attracts players from a wide area.

Walk B - Banbury Street (part), Mill Lane and Mill Street

*This circular walk starts at the War Memorial [A12], proceeds down Banbury Street to the old pump and then continues up Mill Lane and Mill Street to the Village Hall, from where it is only a short stroll back to the Parish Church or War Memorial, a distance of about half a mile. From the old pump **[B9]** the walk can be extended on foot or by car along the Banbury Road to the Edgehill Battle Monument, which is just over one mile away.*

Leaving the War Memorial, the first house on the right-hand side of Banbury Street is

The Bank House [B1], a building existing at the time of the 1774 survey. The present name derives from the activities at the beginning of the 20th century of Charles F Bancroft, a chemist, who also acted as agent for the Metropolitan Bank of England and Wales (later absorbed into the Midland Bank). The black panel which can still be seen on the side of the house once read *C. F. Bancroft, Chemist & Druggist, Depot for Stable, Kennel and General Hunting Requisites*. During the Second World War the building served as a hostel for Land Army girls, and then in the 1950s the basement housed the printing machinery of Gordon Norwood's Roundwood Press (see also **[A6]**). More recently the house has been used by estate agents and an optician.

The Manor Lane bakery. Fred Baker and his first delivery van in the 1930s.

A bakery was added to the back of Bank House in 1860 and continued baking bread until 1970. In the 20th century the bakers here included Frederick Plummer whose son George was killed in 1917 while serving with the Warwickshire Yeomanry in Palestine, and Miss Ada Bloxham, who in 1934 was succeeded by the aptly named Frederick Baker. In 1961 the Leamington Spa Courier reported that "Thursday is always a red-letter day, for that is the day when Kineton's own baker - Fred Baker - has his 'penny bun' day". In addition to two modern steam ovens Fred Baker was still using an ancient coal oven which had been in the bakery for as long as anyone could remember. Easter was a particularly busy time with the making of thousands of Hot Cross Buns for which people would queue from six o'clock on a Good Friday morning. Many family turkeys were brought here on Christmas Day to be cooked in Fred Baker's oven. The oven door remains, but now Kineton has no baker and the Old Bakery is a private house.

Further down on the left of the road is

Londis [B2], formerly known as Greenhill's Stores. There was a shop here in 1774, which was leased to William Woodley, Excise Officer and watchmaker. In 1885 Arthur Rouse bought the property and, in partnership with William Edward Coles, established 'Rouse and Coles', who traded as family grocers and wine, spirit and beer merchants. In the summer months they did a brisk trade taking barrels of Harvest Beer from the Hook Norton Brewery direct to the hay or harvest fields where, after a normal day's work elsewhere, men would give their help in return for copious amounts of ale. After the First World War the business was acquired by Greenhill's Stores Limited, who were already established with a grocery store in Shipston-on-Stour, and it traded in Kineton as Greenhill's Stores for more than sixty years. Continuous ownership since 1885 has meant that the shop has not had a period of closure for well over 100 years.

Arthur Rouse's grocery shop, Banbury Street, about 1918.

Further down the road is

The Carpenter's Arms [B3], which is the most recent of Kineton's public houses, although the site was occupied by a woolcomber's cottage shop in 1774. Whilst the New Inn, Red Lion, Rose and Crown, and Swan all held licences as "an inn, alehouse and victualling house", the 1872 licence for the Carpenters's Arms was only for "beer and cider to be consumed on the premises". This licence was held by Charles Duckett who was able to combine beer retailing with osier growing. In 1892, ownership of the premises was transferred to Flower and Sons, the Stratford-upon-Avon brewers.

On the opposite side of the road,

The present Post Office [B4], occupies a building previously used by Lloyds Bank. Originally this bank, like the predecessor of the Midland bank at the start of this walk, was an agency run by a tradesman, in this case, an ironmonger, Thomas Griffin. It later became a sub-branch, with its own manager living on the premises. One of the best remembered of these managers was John Griffin, who served for many years as Chairman of the Parish Council and Treasurer to the Parish Charities. Lloyds Bank moved to purpose-built premises next door in 1969 and the Post Office was transferred here from Bridge Street by Gerald Price-Rees.

A little further down is

Heronwood House [B5], formerly known as Craddocks, after George Craddock, seedsman and florist of the 1880s. He had a large garden hidden behind the long high wall stretching beyond the wellingtonia. The house is best remembered as the home of the sister of the 18th Lord Willoughby de Broke, the Hon. Mabel Verney, who died here in 1937 at the age of 81. A redoubtable person, her obituaries paid tribute to "a life of service to others", particularly the people of Kineton.

A keen lover of cricket, Miss Verney attended most of the home matches of the Kineton club, and entertained the teams to tea. Local residents with long memories recall that she often brewed the tea outside, over a fire made from sticks she collected from around the sides of the cricket field. Addressing the club in 1912 she told the members that they should not play for the sake of a pleasant afternoon and tea, but for the game itself; indeed, at home matches, she made no secret of wanting the tea interval to be made shorter. At the same cricket club meeting, she took the opportunity to express her determined anti-suffragette views - "if the suffrage movement ever comes to pass it will be because men have got too soft".

There is reason to believe that this house is built on the site of another of Kineton's old public houses, the Woolpack Inn, which was in existence before 1774. At the request of the Parish Vestry the licensee, Mary King, agreed in 1809 to give one night's lodging to paupers travelling through Kineton and in return the Parish Officers agreed to ensure that this activity would not threaten her licence.

On the opposite side of the road, behind the fish-and-chip shop (which has previously housed a blacksmith and a cycle dealer) is the reputed site of

The Railway Inn [B6]. Recalling memories of Kineton in the period 1870-1880, William Rawlins wrote of

> a Blacksmith Shop to which I carried many a ploughshare to be sharpened. The red brick house at back of the Blacksmith Shop was a fully licensed Public House, having a large sign in a square iron frame on a tall wooden post just above the gate where you go to the house. The sign was the 'Railway Inn'. Along the bank at top of garden was a 'Skittle Alley' and many times I watched 'Navvies' playing skittles, the railway being just commenced to be made at this time.

Continue down the road to

Grimes House [B7], which bears the date 1925 and is named after Samuel (Sammy) P Grimes, who ran a hardware and ironmonger's shop there for nearly fifty years. Active in many areas of Kineton life, including the Parish Council where he topped the poll in the first contested election for sixty years, he is particularly remembered for his support of the Kineton Cricket Club and for his generosity to a variety of causes. To mark VE Day in 1945, he organised a party for 200 children in the WI Hall, giving each child sixpence; 250 children were also "entertained to a sumptuous tea" to mark VJ Day.

Across the road is a track leading down to

The Pack Bridge [B8] across the River Dene, and giving access to 'Big Field', once a place of recreation for Kineton people, though ploughed up in the Second World War for the war effort. There was a bridge of some sort here at the time of the 1792 Enclosure Award but the crossing is probably much earlier than this, and may have lain on the footpath to Radway or the bridleway to Westcote, a manor further along Edge Hill. Kineton Albion football team used the 'Big Field' as their ground. It is still the starting point for popular summer walks to the right along the Dene to the Sports and Social Club or to the left along the allotments and across the panoramic track to the Red Road.

Back on the main road, facing the attractive row of grey stone cottages,

A Pump [B9] is the last visible reminder of the time when the inhabitants of Kineton were "amply supplied with water from wells, supplemented by water from the springs on Pittern Hill". In the 19th century there was a road down the bank behind the pump which led to the 'Church Well', which is now covered up. Here horses and cows could drink and the locals draw their water. This well was fed by the underground stream that comes from the fields between the Warwick and Lighthorne roads, supplying several other wells on the way, including one under the old Corn Mill in Mill Lane.

During the 1880s, there was increasing concern about health hazards from polluted wells and the insufficient supply of water from the springs during dry seasons; but it was not until late 1889 that the ratepayers of Kineton and the public health authority could agree on a sufficiently effective but inexpensive remedy. The whole village was then supplied along a network of new pipes with water from tanks on Pittern Hill.

Below the pump and stretching along the river Dene between the allotments and the Banbury Road are

The Osier Beds [B10], where willow was once grown for basket making. Over the years many osier growers and basket makers are listed in the trade directories of the time, including Martin Wisdom, "basket maker and fishmonger" in 1850, and Charles Duckett of the

Carpenter's Arms, "beer retailer and osier grower" in the early 1900s The process is vividly remembered by William Rawlins.

> The osier bed was cultivated at this time [the 1870s] and rented by a man by name Henry Lines, who used to devote his whole time to the business of keeping trenches clean and planting young osiers. The process of the harvesting of the osiers was as follows. In the spring, just when the osiers began to shoot in bud, they was cut and sorted and tied in bundles according to the variety, there being three varieties. After being bundled, they was carried into a pit full of water, the men walking along a plank laid across the pit and standing the bundles on the butt-end upright into the water, which would be about eighteen inches up the bundle. They would remain there till the sap was well up the osier and the peel would run well from the osier. For the peeling process, the owner would now engage about three or four women to assist him. When peeled they were now placed in the sun to dry, and I remember seeing them set on the footpath by the brick wall opposite the old 'Osier Shop' to dry. They was then tied up in bundles again and put in the dry again ready for sale.

Osier workers

From this point it is possible to continue the walk by crossing the road and turning left up Mill Lane, or to extend it along the Banbury Road.

Banbury Road Extension
On the left of the road, about 200 yards from the pump is

Kineton High School [B11, on Area Map only], which provides secondary education for over 1000 young people aged 11-18 from an area which stretches from Ettington to Fenny Compton. Some of the site includes an area of land previously known as Short Acres, a name which has been preserved in part of the adjacent 1970s housing development.

About one mile from the High School, on the left hand side of the B4086, Banbury Road, in a field to the north west of the second bridge out of Kineton is the site of

A Romano-British Settlement [B12, on Area Map only]. This is the earliest known Roman site in the immediate vicinity, but little is known about its origins. Roman and Saxon pottery, some local, some imported from Italy, has been unearthed here. Coins have also been found, the earliest of which date from AD 41-54, though most are of the 3rd and 4th centuries.

A little further towards Banbury, on the right-hand side of the B4086, and with a small lay-by opposite is

The Monument to the Battle of Edgehill [Off both maps], unveiled on Sunday 23 October 1949. It commemorates the battle, the first of the Civil War, which was fought 307 years earlier, on Sunday 23 October 1642. It stands where Parliamentarian Sir James Ramsey's cavalry wing took up position at the start of the battle. A metal plaque states that many of those who lost their lives in the battle are buried three quarters of a mile to the south of this point, at the reputedly haunted Grave Ground Coppice. A similar monument was erected there, but it is now within the Ammunition Depot land and not accessible to the public.

The Edgehill Monument

Kineton from the Banbury Road in the early 1900s.

Returning to the old pump and turning up Mill Lane, there is on the right, the entrance to

Green Farm End and Shortacres. This 1970s housing development is built on the site of Green Farm and on land that was until then ridge and furrow. The farm buildings were in existence in 1774 and the farm was outlined in the 1792 Enclosure award. Particulars for a sale in 1902 described Green Farm as

> a Small Copyhold Estate of about 76 acres, including 31 acres of pasture suitable for Dairying and Young Cattle. The above commends itself very forcibly to Hunting Men, as well as to Investors, being easily converted into a first-class hunting Establishment. Two fields are eminently situated as sites for the erection of Hunting Boxes, for which there is a great demand in this immediate neighbourhood.

These extravagant claims failed to tempt any appropriate purchasers - the hunting boxes did not materialise and dairy farming continued until the mid-1960s. In 1953 the last farmer, Mr Lewis Smart, advertised in the local paper, the Kineton Echo, as a producer of "Tuberculin Tested Channel Island, finest quality milk. Families waited on daily, and Schools supplied". The farmhouse and dairy were attached to the eastern end of the row of cottages which can be seen a little further up Mill Lane opposite the Mill.

The large brick building on the corner of the road was

The Steam Corn Mill [B13]. This large brick building was erected in the middle of the 19th century, and for well over one hundred years was connected with the corn trade. It developed

33

from a simple flour mill, changed hands, and eventually became the premises of a corn merchant. Sited as it was at the centre of an agricultural area, and surrounded by hunting country where hundreds of horses were kept, animal feedstuffs were so much in demand that a fleet of lorries traded daily with the Avonmouth docks, loading and unloading at the brick platform still just visible outside the smaller door. Since the business closed in 1968 the building has been used for storage and packing by various firms, but some old stabling can still be seen through the gates at its side.

Turn left at the Mill. Keep to left until Mill Street is reached, then turn right. About 175 yards to the right is

The Village Hall [B14], which was built in 1986 as the result of an extensive community fund-raising effort. It offers a meeting place for a wide range of village activities, from drama to bingo. The well-equipped building replaces the Women's Institute Hall, which was based on a large World War I hut and had opened in 1924 on land once known as Poor Man's Close. The WI Hall served all sections of the village throughout its existence, even having a billiard room, run by an "Approved Committee of Men". In 1935 the monthly Petty Sessions Court was moved here from the Public Hall **[D1]**, and, with the outbreak of the Second World War, the hall served in turn as a school for evacuees from Coventry, a soldiers' mobile canteen, and a YMCA canteen under the supervision of Lady Willoughby de Broke. After the war the hall was used by the village school for 'school dinners', and on Friday evenings at 7.30 pm there was an opportunity to see such films as *The Man in the White Suit* and *The Lady with the Lamp* by courtesy of the Warwickshire Mobile Cinema.

Walk C - Southam Street and the Market Square

This walk starts from the churchyard gate and proceeds along the length of Southam Street, taking in the Market Square on the way, and ends by the Kineton Cemetery, a distance of about half a mile. Much of this walk can be followed using the map enlargement on page 39.

Turn left to the T-junction. On the opposite side of the road are two shops of particular interest.

A shop with a decorative carved frontage. [C1]. The shop front was moved to this position in 1916, and at present it forms the window of 'Country Pursuits', a shop which, though only recently established, epitomises Kineton's links with the world of horses and riding. Originally the frontage was on the grocer's shop at Dene House, Bridge Street **[A6]** and can be seen in its former position in the illustration on page 21. For many years the Chandler's grocery business, the 'Central Stores', was affectionately called the 'Fortnum and Mason's' of South Warwickshire.

To the left is the building erected as

The Liberal Club [C2]. A small plaque inscribed 'BK 1889' can be seen above the door. This commemorates Bolton King (1860-1937), a pioneer of university settlements and other

Southam Street. The Liberal Club, the Midland Bank and the Central Stores.

social movements. He was born at nearby Chadshunt, and came to school in Kineton before going to Eton when he was twelve. He stood as the Liberal candidate for the Stratford Constituency in 1901 and became Director of Education for Warwickshire from 1904 to 1928. He built a number of model cottages and a reading room in Gaydon, and gave this building in Kineton as a Liberal Club. It was intended that the clubroom should serve as a place

> where a man could spend a comfortable evening, could have his pipe and read the papers or books, or have his game of cards.

At the opening Liberal Bolton King could not refrain from ironically contrasting this with another nearby club for the

> so-called improvement of the Kineton people, which had a good old Tory flavour about it and quite a touching devotion to those good old constitutional institutions, the gin bottle and the beer barrel.

It is not recorded whether the members of the recently opened Conservative Working Men's Club in the centre of the Market Square recognised such a description!

Turn left along Southam Street. On the left is

Chestnut Cottage [C3], a low single storey building, which was a butcher's shop and slaughter house in the early part of the 20th century.

A little further on, set back to the left, is

The Roman Catholic Church [C4], dedicated, like its predecessor in Bridge Street [A4], to St Francis of Assisi. It stands on land which was once part of the vicarage garden. The present building was designed by Brian A Rush and Associates of Kings Norton to replace the smaller church in Bridge Street, and was erected by the Kineton firm of R Brisker and Sons, whose work around the village includes the Methodist Church Schoolroom across the road and the Fire Station on the Warwick Road. The completed building was handed over to the Diocese of Birmingham in October 1975. The altar and furnishings were transferred from Bridge Street and the benches came from a chapel demolished by the Warwick Hospital Authority. The Presbytery was originally in the Market Square, but in 1993 it transferred to Anvil House, and the cottage next door was purchased for use as Parish Rooms.

The 'new' Roman Catholic Church.

Across the road, facing up the triangular green,

Fyfe Lodge [C5] is believed to have become the first freehold house in Kineton when, in 1616, William Austrey received the freehold from the Lord of the Manor, Peter Aylworth. In 1774 the house was owned by John Chandler, the innkeeper of the nearby Swan, and when the house was offered for auction at the Red Lion in 1817, it was described as "a brick and tiled house, butchers shop, malthouse, outbuildings and extensive yard with stables and small garden near the same". The stables and garden were situated on the other side of Southam Street, and were later sold to the Rev. Francis Miller and incorporated into the vicarage garden. In 1911 the newly formed Kineton Tennis Club was offered the use of the private tennis courts attached to the property.

Facing across the green are

Woodfields [C6] and Oddfellows Cottages [C7]. Although the present buildings were obviously built at different times and are now quite separate, they share land which in the 1500s was part of a large private area separate from the village common land. Such an area is properly called a 'close', a word still in use to describe the quiet greens of a 'cathedral close'. In 1774 the land was being rented by David Winter, butcher, from the Earl of Warwick. Much later, in the 19th century, a strip of this close was sold to the King John's Castle Lodge of Oddfellows, a Friendly Society active in Kineton, who built four cottages here. On the southern section of the close two other cottages were joined together and are now known as 'Woodfields', after the family of blacksmiths at Forge House **[C9]**.

At the end of the green is

The Methodist Church [C8]. The first Wesleyan chapel in Kineton was registered for worship on 10 October 1842. John Wesley probably never came to Kineton, but is known to have preached in nearby Oxhill. Two Oxhill farmers full of enthusiasm for his way of worship were among those involved in the acquisition of the piece of land in Southam Street. By 1846 Kineton was on the Banbury Circuit Preaching Plan and by 1858 had become the main church in the Kineton Circuit. Ten years later a vestry was added to the simple rectangular building at a cost of £43. In 1893 the original building, still not large enough, was replaced by the present

Southam Street and the Methodist Church towards the beginning of the 20th century.

structure, and on 21 June a great ceremony marked the laying of the fourteen stones, still clearly bearing the names of local residents. Among them were the minister, the Reverend Samuel Kirk, Bolton King, and Margaret (Maggie) Fisher, wife of Joseph Fisher, the Bridge Street draper and Methodist preacher. The building was finished by the end of the year. Not until 1954 was a schoolroom added, the work being done by Briskers, the local building firm mentioned above. Further alterations have made the building easily accessible to the elderly and disabled, and the interior has been made less austere. Further information can be found in the booklet *The Kineton Methodists 1842-1993*, by David Gill, written to mark the centenary of the present building.

Cross the road again to

Forge House [C9]. The cluster of houses around here all commemorate the use of the area for traditional blacksmith's work. In 1774 two cottages stood on this site, one opening on to Southam Street and the other on to Market Square. Early in the 19th century Daniel Woodfield converted the two into a blacksmith's shop with the anvil located in the back yard. The smithy lasted through more than 100 years of occupation by the Woodfield family, whose name is recalled in the house opposite **[C6]**. From 1911 the Walker family continued the tradition until the death of Jack Walker in 1966.

Blacksmith Jack Walker at work in Southam Street.

Turn immediately left into

The Market Square, the origin of which stems from the charters granted to Stephen de Segrave in 1227 and 1229. The medieval market area may not have been as confined by housing as it is today, and probably extended to the edge of the churchyard. A weekly market was held here on Tuesdays for centuries, but in 1835 it was reported that "the market, which was formerly a very considerable one for grain, has nearly fallen into disuse"; by 1841 it was "unattended" and the Market House had been replaced by a school.

Fairs were held twice a year, in February and in October. The St Paul's Day Fair on 5 February was mainly for seed and corn, and in later years oranges were sold cheaply. 'Orange Day' was discontinued in 1940, no doubt due to lack of imported fruit after several months of war. The fair on 2 October, mainly for cattle and cheese, became a 'Mop' for the hiring of farm labourers and domestic servants and still continues in a small way as a fun fair.

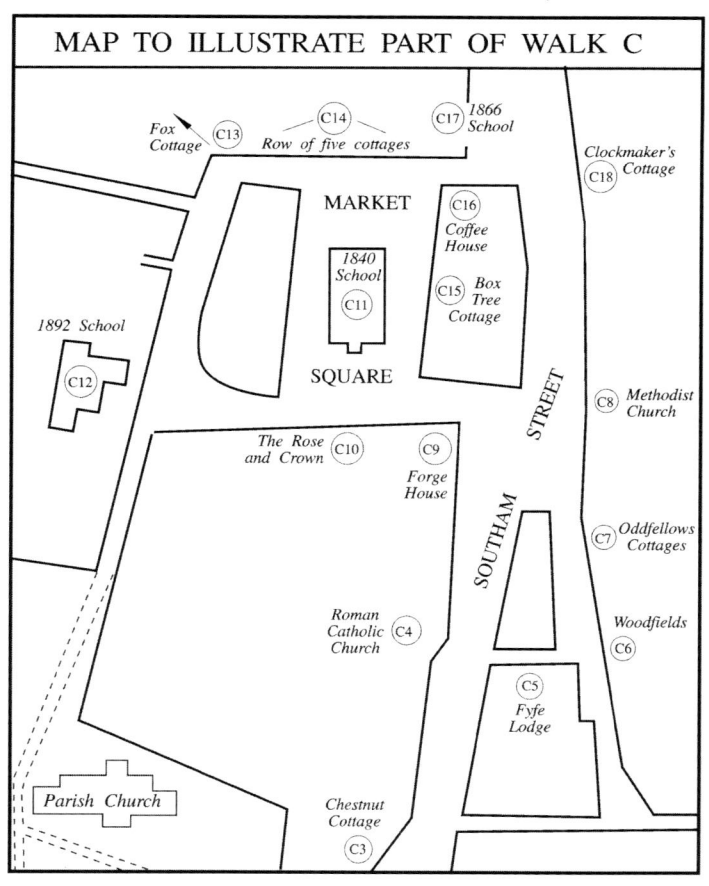

MAP TO ILLUSTRATE PART OF WALK C

- Fox Cottage (C13)
- Row of five cottages (C14)
- 1866 School (C17)
- Clockmaker's Cottage (C18)
- MARKET SQUARE
- 1840 School (C11)
- Coffee House (C16)
- Box Tree Cottage (C15)
- 1892 School (C12)
- The Rose and Crown (C10)
- Forge House (C9)
- Methodist Church (C8)
- Oddfellows Cottages (C7)
- Roman Catholic Church (C4)
- Woodfields (C6)
- Fyfe Lodge (C5)
- SOUTHAM STREET
- Parish Church
- Chestnut Cottage (C3)

The Rose and Crown Inn and the school building in use from 1892 to 1990.

The house half-way up on the left of the square was once

The Rose and Crown Inn [C10]. The lintel above the door bears the date 1664, and there is still a bracket for the inn sign higher up the wall. When offered for sale in 1873, it was described as an "old-established public-house, well situated for business, with good stabling and all necessary conveniences". At one point it was used for meetings of discontented agricultural labourers, at least one of which was attended by Joseph Arch, the Primitive Methodist local preacher from Barford. He became their champion, was elected to parliament, and founded the National Agricultural Labourers' Union. The building ceased to be a public-house in the 1960s, and for some time was the Roman Catholic Presbytery.

Those interested in education will want to read the history of schools in Kineton included in part 3, for there is room for only a brief summary in this walk. It will soon become obvious that this small area of Kineton seems to have been associated with education for a long time.

Opposite the Rose and Crown, the brick building in the centre of the square was

The first purpose-built School. [C11] The present building replaced the old market house, and opened in 1840 as a school for 110 boys and girls. It was there that Mrs Caroline Blunt, Kineton's first 'headmistress' was to shape the education of the village children for over fifty years, while herself raising a family of five. When the premises became inadequate as a school, Lord Willoughby de Broke offered the building for use as a Working Men's Club, while in the 1970s and 1980s it served as the public library. The Kineton Volunteer Fire Brigade kept their engine at the back of the building for three-quarters of a century until 1955.

The walk continues to the left, towards the

School building of 1892 [C12], now a doctor's surgery. The Stratford Herald described the new school as

> built in the Elizabethan style, of red brick with Edge Hill stone dressings. On each side of the entrance porch are the lobbies and lavatory, the latter being fitted with excellent arrangements - almost too good, we think, for school use.

Nevertheless this 'excellent' lavatory contained only washbasins until 1988 when the outdoor toilets for pupils were closed. The school building, in use for almost a century, finally closed two years later.

From here turn right along the narrow road. In the north-west corner of the square can be seen two brick pillars with stone foxes on them. This is the entrance to

Fox Cottage [C13], a private residence. There was a cottage on this site at the time of the 1774 survey, adjacent to others on fields at the corner of the Market Square. By 1806 it had become "a dwelling house with a newly built, three-stall stable, outbuildings and garden or pleasure ground containing 1000 square feet with a wall around it." A sale notice of 1813 described this wall as 11 feet high with 14 inch feet. In the 1950s the 20th Lord Willoughby de Broke built a new house here, which he named Fox Cottage, incorporating the walled garden mentioned in 1806. He also retained one of the other cottages, renaming it Vixen Hall. In 1981 the property was purchased by Hilton Newton-Mason, who further developed it by enlarging the garden, incorporating a spectacular waterfall which he had purchased from the Chelsea Flower Show.

On the north side of the square, facing towards the former 'Rose and Crown', is

A row of five cottages [C14], with dormers, mullioned windows, and drip stones. The date 1674 has been scratched above the stone doorway of the present No.1. During the 1860s the property was bought by the Rev Francis Miller, who pulled down a malthouse and built a school on the corner with Southam Street **[C17]**. One house was retained as the schoolmaster's home. Two others were leased to William Osborne, baker, one of which is still called 'The Old Cottage Bakery'.

On the east side of the square, backing on to Southam Street, are buildings showing remains of 17th-century timber framing. In the centre of these is

Box Tree Cottage [C15], dated 1582.

Kineton: The Village and its History

On the left, with its slightly jettied upper storey, is

The Coffee House [C16]. By 1810 this building was being used as a public house known as the New Inn, and continued as such until 1880. On the death of the owner in that year the licensing magistrates refused to grant a new licence "on the grounds that there were sufficient Public Houses in Kineton." Under the patronage of Georgiana, Lady Willoughby de Broke, the former New Inn was reopened in the following year as a coffee tavern

> intended as a place of resort for the workmen and labourers of the town and neighbourhood instead of frequenting public-houses.

The large parlour was used as a reading-room, while another room served as a coffee and refreshment room; there were also bedrooms provided for lodgers and a room "devoted to females." One of the additional services offered by the Coffee House was a register for young girls seeking situations; there was a penny registration fee and an additional charge of one shilling if work was found.

Joseph Chandler with pupils at the village school.

Return to Southam Street by the side of the Coffee House. Immediately to the left, notice another

School building of 1866 [C17], now converted to private housing. Although it served for some thirty years as the village school, many of Kineton's older residents refer to the building as 'The Parish Rooms'. Set in a narrow cupboard, a feature of the school was the "naughty boys' cage," the remains of which were removed to the back of the Parish Church. In 1876 the headmaster recorded

> Put Samuel Capp into the cage for truant playing. At 12.15 and before I had left the school, the door being unlocked, his mother came in, went to the cage and released him saying at the same time 'her child should not be locked up' or words to that effect. I allowed him to go home but refused to receive him into school again except at the Vicar's hands.

It had been a bad week for the poor headmaster, and he submitted his resignation the same day!

On the opposite side of Southam Street, at No 8, is

Clockmaker's Cottage [C18]. Although it is thought that, for a time at the beginning of the 19th century, this cottage housed a school for the poor of the parish run by a churchwarden, it derives its present name from its association with the Wade family. Robert Wade (died 1892) and his son, Henry William Wade (died 1943), between them carried on the business of watch and clock making for more than seventy years. The order for the clock on the parish church was given to Robert in 1884, and he was made responsible for its care and management. Both Robert and William were also contracted to maintain the clocks for the local railway company.

Continue along Southam Street away from the village centre. Fork left up the Lighthorne Road, where, in about 100 yards, just before the bridge that crosses the disused railway line, is

A lozenge-shaped metal Weight Restriction Sign [C19], erected by the Stratford-upon-Avon and Midland Junction Railway Company under the Motor Car Acts 1896 and 1903 to warn that "This bridge is insufficient to carry a Heavy Motor Car". The weight-limit is no longer specified, but until the early 1980s it carried, surprisingly, a wartime Class 40 (Light-Tank) Sign.

Now return to Southam Street and turn left towards Gaydon. A little further on, to the right of the road

Fighting Close is a small housing development of the late 1970s built round a large house which dates from the early 20th century. It takes its name from the field where competitive fighting used to take place at the time of the Mop Fair each October and where the fair people had to stay until they were allowed into the Market Square. A diary entry for 1851 records

> Kineton Mop, small attendance, not much fighting nor much hiring: poor mop with the surgeons.

On the right, just beyond the roundabout, is the entrance to

Kineton Cemetery [C20], which was opened as an extension to the churchyard surrounding the Parish Church, on land given by Lord Willoughby de Broke and consecrated in 1946. In the first row of the cemetery are the graves of two notable residents of Bridge Street. One was Admiral Sir Walter Cowan, and the other the Honourable Patience Hanbury, daughter of the 18th Lord Willoughby de Broke.

Walk D - Warwick Road

This walk starts from the churchyard gate and proceeds to King John's Mound, a distance of less than half a mile. The walk can be extended on foot or by car along Brookhampton Lane or up Pittern Hill.

Come out of the churchyard and turn right towards Wellesbourne. On the right is

The Public Hall [D1]. There were buildings here in 1774, when the land belonged to the Lord of the Manor, the Earl of Warwick. Thomas Griffin, who had come to Kineton in 1872 to take over a long-established ironmongery business previously run by Josiah Woodley and Daniel Walker, bought the site in 1886. He pulled down a malt house on the site and erected the Public Hall, with shop premises on the ground floor. The inscription above the ground-floor windows is the only remaining indication of the building's original function. Opened in 1894, the hall had a stage and gallery, with dressing rooms and ante-rooms attached, and could seat nearly 300 people. Until the Second World War it was used for balls, public meetings and other entertainments, and was also the venue for the monthly meeting of the Petty Sessions Court where minor offences could be dealt with locally. By 1912, with great foresight, the ironmongery business underneath had been extended to include a garage, which continued as

The Kineton Garage under the Public Hall, Warwick Road.

the Kineton Garage into the 1980s. In more recent years much of the building has been converted into private housing known as Church Mews.

A little further on

Haven House [D2], is now a residential home for the elderly. It was first erected in about 1750 by a farmer, Robert Croft, on land known as Providence Close. For many decades it was called Woodley House after Josiah Woodley (1805-1887) who purchased the copyhold property in 1833 and enlarged and improved it. Not only was Josiah Woodley successful in business as a maltster, clock and watch maker, ironmonger, corn dealer, land agent and auctioneer, but, according to his Stratford Herald obituary, he also took "an active interest in every movement for advancing the interests of the town and making its social life more enjoyable". For years he was known in the village as "the Mayor of Kineton", though exactly when and why he gained this honorary title is not clear.

In 1891 the property was purchased by the 18th Lord Willoughby de Broke and was used by various members of his family; after the sale of the Compton Verney estate in 1921 it became, for thirty years, the family's principal local residence. During the early years of the Second World War a machine gun company of the Czech Army was billeted in the house.

On the opposite side of the road is

Roxburgh House [D3], now another residential home for the elderly. In November 1862 the Warwick Advertiser reported that

> through the munificence of Lady Willoughby de Broke, a handsome building has been erected at the entrance to the town on the Warwick road, part of which when completed will be appropriated to the use of the Literary Society as a library and reading room, and occasionally for lectures and concerts, the other part being intended as a school for the middle classes, which will be of great advantage to the town and neighbourhood.

The library was removed in 1877, when the school required the space for a dining room, but Kineton Middle Class School continued here with varying degrees of success until the early 1920s. More recently the building was divided and served as both a private dwelling and, until the 1950s, the Willoughby de Broke Estate Office.

Returning to the right hand side of the road, the house (Rossmore) with the prominent stone doorway was

Kineton's first Police Station [D4]. Although there was a jail in Kineton in 1166, it was only in 1858, following the establishment of the Warwickshire Constabulary just one year before, that the building of this station was started. The design is very similar to those in Henley-in-Arden and Kenilworth. In 1874 the premises consisted of three cells and a house for

The first Police Station in Warwick Road

the Inspector, John Lapworth, and were the centre for police activities in the surrounding villages. During the 1950s the police station was moved to a new building opposite Station Garage and in 1995 to Wellesbourne.

Cross the entrance to King John's Road to reach the site of

The Gas Works [D5]. Although Kineton no longer has a mains gas supply, the village had its own gas works from 1863 until about 1948 on land which now forms the entrance to Little Pittern. The house on the right was that of the gas works manager, and behind it, now demolished, stood two gasholders. In its day the works served Kineton, Combroke and Lord Willoughby de Broke's estate at Compton Verney. The supply was presumably fairly satisfactory, though people alive in Kineton today who remember the last days of the gas works still joke about its unreliability. They also recall the gas holders looking "like porcupines, they were so full of sticks coated in red lead filling the rust holes." There is little doubt that a vast injection of capital would have been needed to update the works. Many regret that the private gas works was never absorbed under nationalisation, with the result that at the time of writing only bottled gas is available in Kineton.

On the opposite side of the road can be seen

The Fire Station [D6], which was formally opened by the 20th Lord Willoughby de Broke in 1955. Before this the Kineton fire engine had been kept at the back of the building in the centre of the Market Square. This was the time of a horse-drawn fire pump. No horse was kept

The Parish Church and Five Walks Round Kineton

at the station, and as the number of horses stabled in the village became fewer, so the brigade's effectiveness was reduced by the need to go as far as Butlers Marston for a horse! This state of affairs continued until 1931 when things improved greatly with the introduction of a motorised fire engine, and even more with a purpose-built station in the Warwick Road.

The Fire Brigade in the Warwick Road.

A little further on, turn left and walk down Castle Road, opposite Station Garage. At the end is the entry to

King John's Mound [D7], now a scheduled Ancient Monument. This is a 'Motte and Bailey' built in the 12th or early 13th century. It stands on high ground covering what was probably the main crossing of the River Dene on an early route from London to Warwick via Banbury and Ratley. As Kineton was king's land, it could have been constructed by Stephen during the time of the invasion by Matilda of Anjou in 1139 or by John during his troubles with the Barons before 1215. There are several other sites in the area which carry his name, so it seems likely that it was built for King John. Legend also relates that he held a Court Leet here. The Motte and Bailey system (a protected keep and enclosed area for people and animals) was brought into Britain by the Normans. Initially the strongpoint would have been surrounded by wooden pallisades, but some were later strengthened with thick stone walls, as at Warwick and Nottingham. King John's Castle in Kineton was never castellated and clearly fell into early disuse. Over the centuries the Motte has slowly eroded to well below its original height, but lately the Parish Council, which owns the site, has cleared much of the undergrowth, revealing the outline of the Bailey.

Kineton: The Village and its History

Return to the Warwick Road and turn left. To the left of the road, with its entrance opposite Station Garage, was

The Railway Station [D8], although it is hard to find any trace of it today. The road still crosses the bridge over the long disused line. A light industrial estate now covers the site of what seems, from photographs, to have been a pretty, well-kept station. There was a double track, with 'up' and 'down' platforms, and a signal box with sophisticated equipment. The main buildings were on the 'down', or south, side, with goods yard and coal sidings behind. The station first opened in 1871, but after only six years it was in such difficulty financially that it was closed to passenger traffic and open only for freight. The Kineton parish magazine of 1883 had quite a lot to say about its shortcomings

> We wonder whether (if the trains do run again) you will be able to stop the train at any given point by waving a newspaper, and whether the man in a hurry will again prefer walking. A good shaking is good for a torpid liver. If this is correct, those who suffer from such sluggishness will certainly benefit by a journey on this line, which will afford them such a shaking as it would be difficult, if not impossible, to get in any other part of the British Isles.

Despite such sarcasm the railway was refinanced, opened again to passengers in 1885, and survived this time until 1952, when it finally closed to passenger traffic. The freight line closed after a further eleven years.

Kineton Railway Station in the early 1900s

From this point it is possible to return to the centre of the village along the Warwick Road or to extend the walk in one of two ways:-

Extension 1 - Brookhampton Lane [Area Map only]
After crossing the old railway bridge, turn left into Brookhampton Lane, and after about 350 yards, there is on the right the site of

King John's Well [D9]. Today little can be seen of this well, marked on many maps, except an occasional trickle across the road. In the middle of the 19th century guide books claimed that the inhabitants were amply supplied with water from wells and that strangers were shown a spring called 'King John's Well'. The well later became part of Kineton's mains water system, with the water being pumped up the hill to a large tank and then distributed by means of iron mains and lead service pipes to houses on the principal streets. The remains of this and later holding tanks are clearly marked on the Ordnance Survey map and can seen by taking the nearby public footpath over the stile and up the hill.

Half a mile further on, at the very end of Brookhampton Lane, lies Brookhampton Farmhouse and the site of

Brookhampton Village [Off Maps]. Brookhampton was originally part of Kineton, but became a separate Manor in 1199, when King John gave the land to the Trublevill family. It was clearly a thriving community during the Middle Ages. Outlines of buildings and the pattern of ridge and furrow farming can be seen in aerial photographs. It appears that the village was largely depopulated in the 14th century, almost certainly due to the Black Death. Today all that remains of the community is Brookhampton Farmhouse, the original manor house, parts of which date back to the 15th or 16th century.

Returning 175 yards towards Kineton, in a field on the right-hand side opposite the turning to Pittern Hill Farm, is the site of a

Roman Villa [Off Maps]. Although nothing can be seen on the surface today, the outlines of the foundations of a substantial villa are clearly visible in aerial photographs. During ploughing many Roman coins and fragments of pottery have been unearthed in the area.

Extension 2 - Pittern Hill and Compton Verney.
Half-way up Pittern Hill, on the left-hand side of the road, just after the footpath crosses to that side, is a

Milepost [D10], showing the distances to London (86 miles), Banbury (13 miles), and Stratford and Warwick (both 10 miles). It bears the mark of *W. Glover & Sons, Manufacturers,*

The Turnpike milepost on Pittern Hill

Warwick, and is probably associated with the Kineton and Wellesbourne Turnpike Trust which was established in 1770.

At the top of the hill, in a field to the right, can be seen the remains of a

Windmill [Off Maps], the last survivor of a number of such mills which served the village for over 700 years. The barrel-like tower mill, as distinct from an early wooden post mill, was built before 1789, but ceased working in about 1880. The 1792 Enclosure award refers to the site as the 'Windmill Quarter', and certainly the high ground of Pittern Hill is an ideal site for a wind driven mill.

A little further on, also on the right, is the site for the

Millennium Wood [Off Maps], which is being created as a new 8.5 acre woodland area with a variety of broad-leafed trees to mark the year 2000. In time it will go some way to compensate for the loss from Dutch Elm Disease of the famous avenue of elm trees that shaded the road to Compton Verney.

After another mile, on the right, is

Compton Verney House [Off Maps] which, with its park and lakes, was formerly the seat of the Lords Willoughby de Broke. The house has medieval origins but was substantially remodelled in the 18th and 19th centuries. In the 1990s it was rescued from a state of dereliction sby the Compton Verney House Trust, set up by the millionaire Peter Moores. Millions of pounds have been spent on its restoration and conversion to a major art gallery open to the public. It is hoped that the gallery will eventually become a major venue for international art exhibitions, as well as housing Peter Moores' own art collection.

The Parish Church and Five Walks Round Kineton

Walk E - Little Kineton

This short walk can be taken separately by starting on the Green *[E6]* in Little Kineton or as an extension of the Bridge Street Walk - Walk A. Little Kineton is shown on the Area Map only.

If taken as an extension, continue past the Manor Lane turning to the bottom of Bridge Street.

The Bridge [E1] crosses the River Dene, which flows on through Wellesbourne to join the Avon in Charlecote Park. As the street was already known as Bridge Street in 1774, it seems probable that since early times there has been some form of bridge here, possibly only a footbridge. A ford some 150 yards downstream served as the crossing point and was linked to the Warwick Road by tracks which are now obscured by the developments of Park Piece and Shepherd Place. Two bodies, said to be Roundheads killed defending the ford during the Battle of Edgehill, were found in the riverbank in 1853. From the left-hand side of the bridge it is possible to make out the remains of late-Victorian filter tanks which once formed part of Kineton's sewage treatment system.

Beyond, to the left of the road, are

Kineton Sports Field [E2] and the premises of the **Kineton Sports and Social Club**. The building nearest the gateway is the Garland Memorial Pavilion, which previously served as a recreation room at the Clarendon House hospital **[A7]**. It was presented to the Kineton Cricket Club in 1919 "in memory of the Great War." Although the cricket and football clubs had been sharing the field for some years, it was not until 1968 that the prospect of changing facilities for both was offered by the start of further building. Prior to this the headed notepaper of the Kineton United Football Club included the advice: "Ground: Kineton Playing Field - Dressing room: Red Lion".

There was certainly a cricket club in Kineton as early as 1860, when the concluding match of the season was between the married and the single members. Two years later the Warwickshire Advertiser reported that

> The batting and bowling of Lord Willoughby was very good, and there is little doubt but that his lordship will soon become a fine player.

Their confidence in Lord Willoughby de Broke was not misplaced: he became a member of the celebrated 'I Zingari' cricket team, and played sometimes for the Warwickshire County Cricket Club, of which he was a founder.

Home matches were played on a rough pitch on 'Big Field', off the Banbury Road, and on the lawn at Compton Verney House; then, with increasing regularity, at Kineton House **[E3]**. Following the sale of this house to Joshua Fielden in 1911, a new site had to be found. £150 was hurriedly raised by public subscription, to level and equip the present ground for the opening of the 1912 season on land given by Lord Willoughby de Broke.

'Big Field' also saw the opening match of a new football club in 1891, when Kineton beat the Vale of Red Horse FC by four goals to one. Since then, several Kineton football clubs have come and gone, with mixed fortunes. In the 1920s Kineton Albion had several successful seasons, one year gaining three cups and a shield. In 1953 the local paper reported that Kineton Wasps had signed on former international, A J Karminski, Lord Willoughby de Broke's butler and "one of the greatest goal keepers that Poland ever had." Kineton United was formed in 1960, by which time the Albion and the Wasps had been defunct for some years.

The well-equipped Sports and Social Club now includes bowling greens and a hockey field, and caters for a wide range of activities.

Returning to the right hand side of the road, the path bears right to the entrance to the small residential estate known as

Norton Grange [E3], with the Mansion House at its centre, the latest stage in a development that has seen many changes in the last four centuries. When the manor of Little Kineton was acquired by Charles Bentley in the mid-17th century, there was already a fine gabled house with 16 hearths in these grounds. In the 1720s, another Charles Bentley began remodelling and extending the house, and laid out fashionable gardens. Richard Hill, a London tobacco merchant, acquired the manor in 1786; he demolished the old house and started to build a new one. However, when Lord Willoughby de Broke bought the estate in 1823 the house was still unfinished and he subsequently had it pulled down.

Kineton House, Little Kineton, in its days as a home of the Willoughby de Brokes.

Kineton House, which is now known as the Mansion House, was built on another part of the site and remained in the hands of the Willoughby de Brokes until 1911, when it was purchased by Joshua Fielden, the new Joint-Master of the Warwickshire Hunt. An inventory taken in 1911 reveals a flourishing country estate. The 15 main bedrooms and comfortable day rooms were supported by all the traditional service areas of laundry, still room, and gun rooms, and there were some 10 staff bedrooms and accommodation for butler and housekeeper. At their peak the extensive gardens contained palm trees, azaleas, dracaenas, ferns and carnations, and the vegetable gardens supplied a great variety of fruit and vegetables including Muscat grapes. The people of Kineton were welcomed in the gardens for a huge number of school treats and fetes until well after the end of the Second World War.

During both World Wars the house was used as a Red Cross hospital. Then, in 1945, the estate was sold again, this time to the Norton Trust, a Birmingham based charity for delinquent boys, and it became an Approved School with its own farm. In the late 1980s, on the closure of Norton School, the present private residential development began and this still carries the Norton name.

On the Butlers Marston side of the entrance to Norton Grange can be seen

The Kennels [E4] of the Warwickshire Hunt, which were erected in 1839 and were among the earliest purpose-built hunt kennels in the country. They were built

> to contain about 60 couples of good hounds, which have been purchased from some of the best packs in the kingdom; convenient houses are attached for the huntsman and groom.

For many years the Warwickshire Hunt was one of the leading packs in the country, hunting five days a week, attracting wealthy supporters to the area, and contributing significantly to the economy of Kineton.

The late 20th century stone cottages on the opposite side of the main road, facing the entrance to Norton Grange, stand on the site of

The Independent Chapel [E5], which flourished for most of the 19th century and which could seat about 100 worshippers. Originally built by an Anglican clergyman about 1796 "when there was only one service on a Sunday in the Parish Church", it was taken over in 1813 by a group of Dissenters, and ten years later was in the hands of trustees as "a dissenting Place of Worship belonging to the two Denominations of Independents and Baptists". On Sunday, 30 March 1851, it is recorded that 68 adults and children attended the afternoon service. However, attendances gradually declined and the chapel fell into disrepair during the 1880s. It was re-opened as a Congregational chapel in 1890, and enjoyed a brief revival with a minister resident in Kineton, until it finally closed a few years later.

After the Second World War, the chapel building became a storage barn for Norton School's farm, before demolition to make way for the cottages.

At the heart of Little Kineton are

The Green and The Pond [E6], the considerable charms of which are enhanced by the stone-built cottages that overlook them on three sides. In 1909 the Stratford Herald reported that

> A great improvement has been effected at Little Kineton by the levelling of portions of the green and the removal of rubbish therefrom. In addition Lord Willoughby has generously had planted three chestnut trees in a central position, which in years to come will add much to the picturesqueness of this pretty hamlet.

Lord Willoughby de Broke placed the green "at the disposal of the parish council so far as the rights of the Lords of the Manor are concerned" in 1913, and the land is now registered as common land. During the early years of the 20th century the parish council was constantly drawing attention to the dangerous condition of the pool, and in 1919 it seemed likely that it

The pond, Little Kineton

would be filled in. However, it survived and, although sadly its ducks have been removed, it is still a home for moorhens.

The chestnut trees planted in 1909 are now mature, and under them is a Victorian wall post box. The refurbished post box was moved to its present position from the side of the main road in 1977 to celebrate the Silver Jubilee of the reign of Queen Elizabeth II.

On the far side of the Green is the large house now known as

Diana Lodge [E7]. Between the late 1850s and 1883, Kineton Lodge flourished as a school for young boys from upper middle class homes. The headmaster throughout this period was James Hunter, who played a leading role in the cultural and social life of the village. The house became known as Diana Lodge (perhaps after Diana, the goddess of hunting ?) when, in the late 1880s, it was the home of the Honourable Mabel Verney, daughter of the 17th Lord Willoughby de Broke and promoter of many projects to improve the social welfare of Kineton. During the early part of the 20th century it was leased as a hunting-box to a succession of fashionable supporters of the Warwickshire Hunt, who were no doubt attracted by the proximity of the kennels. Among its guests was the Prince of Wales, later to become Edward VIII.

The lane passing between Diana Lodge and Verney Cottages is known as

Red Road. This pretty winding lane was once part of a route from Warwick, via Moreton Morrell, Kineton, Radway and Ratley, to Banbury and thence to London. The name comes from the Saxon word *rad* meaning 'red' and probably describes the colour of the soil in the area at the top of Edgehill. Red Road extends to Radway and to the track up through woods beyond, where it is known as King John's Lane. Some say the name was changed after the battle of Edgehill, when the road ran "red with blood". Certainly in October 1642 the Royalist cavalry used the road to outflank the right of the Parliamentary forces during the Battle of Edgehill and so enter Kineton. Roman coins have been unearthed beside the ancient road. Although Red Road was closed in 1940, when the Ammunition Depot was established on the surrounding farmland, a short stretch remains accessible.

From the Red Road it is possible to take one of the public footpaths or bridleways to the left through to the present Banbury Road via the Pack Bridge [B8], about a mile away. From there it is only a short walk back to the Parish Church.

Chapter 3

The Shaping of a Community:
For those who want to know more

The Manor

Origins of the Manor

Although the precise origins of the manorial system are uncertain, they can be traced back to the settlements formed when people banded together out of common interest or for protection. Such groupings go back to the earliest tribal systems, but were refined for administrative purposes by the Romans and later the Saxons. With the invasion by the Normans the principle of the 'Manor' was established, and was quickly welded into their feudal system. This system was based on the assumption that the king owned all the land in the kingdom and, as a reward for military or monetary services, could use his patronage to bestow defined areas of land, 'Manors', upon his noblemen and key supporters. The aim was to keep these powerful men loyal and to provide the king with money and armed soldiers when needed. The noblemen then became 'Lords of their Manor' and in turn they leased strips of their land to the local inhabitants for housing or cultivation in return for ground rent or services on their lord's private fields.

The Role of the Manor

A manor was not simply an area given to a lord purely for the collection of rents and taxes. It also had a legal and administrative role to perform within the local government organisations of both the county and the hundred. There is a report of a jail being built in Kineton in 1166, although its location remains a mystery. There were originally three levels of court within the Feudal system; the Court Baron, where civil disputes between freeholders were settled; the Court Customary for non-criminal cases among villeins (feudal tenants); and the Court Leet where petty criminals were punished. It seems that a Court Leet was sometimes attended by the Lord of the Manor himself and local legend claims that King John once held a Court Leet at King John's Castle.

During the Middle Ages justice became more centralised, and the Hundred played a greater role and the Manorial Court a lesser one. Petty Sessions, the predecessor of Magistrates Courts, were set up to try minor crimes, and increasingly the Manorial Court was concerned only with the transfer of land. Property and land could be held freehold, as today ; leasehold, where the land was leased from the Lord of the Manor for a defined number of years at a ground rent, with the land reverting to him at the end of that period; or, more often, copyhold, whereby the

The Shaping of a Community

land was leased for 300 years at a ground rent. Copyholders had clearly defined rights : they could build a house on the rented plot, which could be sub-let and passed through the family for a small fee, or the copyhold itself could be sold to a third party, who would have to pay a fee to the Lord of the Manor, but who would then start a fresh 300-year term.

At the beginning of the 19th century only a few houses in Kineton were freehold and not many were leasehold, these being mainly in Market Square. The vast majority were copyhold, when every change of occupant had to be confirmed at the Manorial Court and recorded in the Court Rolls. Many of the rolls for both Kineton Magna and Parva have survived and they detail what was built on each plot and the date when it changed hands.

Henry Verney, 18th Lord Willoughby de Broke, Lord of the Manor 1862-1902

As the 19th century wore on, more and more copyholders purchased their freeholds from Lord Willoughby de Broke. The demise of the copyhold system came finally with the 1922 Law of Property Act, which gave copyholders the undisputed right to purchase their freeholds.

Lords of the Manor

Even before Norman times, Kineton had been held by the king, but it was not until 1216 that King John used royal patronage to bestow the Lordship of Kineton Magna upon Stephen de Segrave. Shortly afterwards, King Henry III gave the Lordship of Kineton Parva (Little Kineton) to Ralph Trublevill, whose son subsequently transferred it to Stephen de Segrave, thus leading to the union of the two manors. The area of the two manors differed from today, for a little earlier, in 1154, part of Little Kineton had been given to Kenilworth Priory, presumably to provide tithes for St Peter's Church which they owned. Stephen de Segrave, by now a significant landowner, realised the financial advantages of running an official market. He obtained royal authority to hold markets and fairs in Kineton, and so laid the foundation for its future prosperity.

Lordships were granted to families in perpetuity, but Nicholas de Segrave, Stephen's grandson, forfeited the lordships in 1260 for supporting an abortive uprising against Henry III. However, the lordships were restored to the family in 1267 at a time when Simon de Montfort's power over England had been destroyed, and the weak government, if not the life, of Henry III was at an end. They remained in Segrave hands until 1353, when they passed by marriage into the Mowbray family. In 1481, again by marriage, the lordships passed to the Berkeley family of Berkeley Castle in southern Gloucestershire. In 1575, Lord Berkeley decided to sell the lordships separately, Kineton Magna to Francis Aylworth, who was his steward there at the time, and Kineton Parva to William Burton. At a stroke, not only had the manors been separated, but for the first time they had been sold rather than received as a gift or by inheritance. The pattern for the future was established.

There is evidence that there were two manor houses, one for each manor, but particularly in Greater Kineton the early lords appear to have been for the most part absentee landlords, needing the houses only for important tenants. Towards the end of the 18th century, the Hill family, though Lords of Little Kineton, lived in Greater Kineton for some years when Richard

Little Kineton House in the 18th century. Drawing by Thomas Ward.

Hill had pulled down the Manor House in Little Kineton and failed to complete its rebuilding. The house he destroyed, known then as the Mansion, had been built, or possibly adapted from an existing house in Little Kineton, by Charles Bentley when he bought the Lordship in 1656. The building was further enhanced by his grandson, another Charles, and by 1720 had become one of Warwickshire's most renowned houses, with extensive and elaborate gardens with a formal canal, wilderness, bowling green, and a 'pleasure garden with clipped trees and a yew pavilion'. The Bentley family became closely involved with Kineton over the years and several handsome monumental slabs can be seen in the chancel of the church, bearing the family coat of arms incorporating a little mermaid.

The Willoughby de Broke family, who re-united the two lordships by purchasing them both early in the 19th century, rebuilt Little Kineton Manor, replacing the house destroyed by Richard Hill with the building that still stands today, albeit much modified, at the centre of Norton Grange [E3]. Compton Verney, the family seat of the Verney family (the Lords Willoughby de Broke) for more than 500 years, remained their main residence, but their association with Kineton was very close. Like the Bentleys before them, they left their mark on the church in the form of memorials and stained glass, endowed and built schools in the village, and took much more than a superficial interest in village organisations. Compton Verney was sold in 1921, and the family came to live in the centre of Kineton, first in Woodley House in Warwick Road (now Haven House) [D2] and later, in Fox Cottage [C13], before moving to London in the 1970s. Most of the manorial land in Kineton and Little Kineton had been sold off by the 1930s but the titles of Lord of the Manor remained and were purchased in 1986 by Baron Kenneth Benfield.

A chronological sequence of all the families owning the manors is to be found overleaf.

Agriculture and Trade

It is obvious from the very earliest documents relating to the village that Kineton has always been an agricultural centre. Its position at the edge of the Vale of the Red Horse, in a bowl of hills bounded to the south by Edgehill and to the north by Pittern Hill, with the little River Dene flowing through it, gives rise to a variety of fertile soils. The low-lying lands of the surrounding Feldon, though marshy in places, have always supported both livestock and the raising of crops to feed the population of an expanding village, and from the 13th to the 19th centuries Kineton market thrived.

Towards Edgehill, on the southern boundaries of the parish, and in several other places on the hillside slopes, it is still possible to see characteristic patterns of ridge-and-furrow in the grass fields. The ridges have survived from the time when the fields were cultivated in strips by the villagers. Since the enclosures, when grass was sown to feed the animals in the newly enlarged fields, they have rarely if ever been ploughed for arable land. Most of the soil in these low lying fields is of blue lias clay, and is heavy and difficult to work. Not until there were better drainage techniques, powerful machinery and modern fertilizers and sprays, could arable crops be grown efficiently.

Chronological Sequence of Lords of the Manor

PERIOD	KINETON MAGNA MANOR Kineton	KINETON PARVA MANOR Little Kineton	KENILWORTH PRIORY LAND Part of Little Kineton
900	?	?	?
950		King Edgar	
1000		Saxon Kings of England	
1050		King Edward, The Confessor	
1100		Norman Kings of England	
1150		Plantagenet Kings of England	1154 Henry II grants some land in Kineton Parva to Kenilworth Priory
1200	1216 John grants Manor to Stephen de Segrave	c1216 Henry III grants Manor to Ralph Trublevill 1233 Henry Trublevill transfers Manor to Stephen de Segrave	
1300			
	1353 Passes to Mowbray Family by marriage		Kenilworth Priory
1400			
	1481 Passes to Berkeley Family by marriage 1492 No male heir in Berkeley Family so reverts to Crown		
1500			1539 Dissolution of Monasteries so land reverts to Crown
	1553 No male heir to Edward VI so reverts to Berkeley Family		1542 Sold by Crown to Robert Burgoyne
	1575 Sold by Lord Berkeley to Francis Aylworth for £500	1575 Sold by Lord Berkeley to William Burton for £720	
1600	1617 Sold by Aylworth Family to Sir Fulke Greville (later Earl of Warwick Family) for £2,000	1596 Sold by Burton Family to Thomas Puckering	Burgoyne Family
1650	Earl of Warwick Family	1656 Sold by Puckering Family to Charles Bentley	1653 Sold by Burgoyne Family to Charles Bentley and incorporated back into Kineton Parva Manor
1700		1784 Sold by Bentley Family to Richard Hill	
1800	1806 Sold by Earl of Warwick to Lord Willoughby de Broke	1823 Sold by Hill Family to Lord Willoughby de Broke	
1850	Lord Willoughby de Broke Family		
1900-2000	1986 - Sold by Lord Willoughby de Broke Family to Baron Kenneth Benfield		

Haymaking, 1910

Many of the fields have been known by the same names for as long as records are available, and to this day reflect not only local landmarks, like Woodside, and Grave Ground, but also the use to which the land was put, like Bean Furlong (on the left side of the Tysoe Road just outside Little Kineton) and Flaxlands (on Pittern Hill). Some areas, especially the low ground to the south of Kineton, were used for cattle; sheep tended to be grazed on the poorer quality banks which were often badly drained, such as Pittern Hill, where scrub bushes and gorse grew amongst the pasture, or in the wetter areas with reeds, down Red Road, for example. Sheep were raised not so much for meat as for the wool clip which was more profitable and could be sold at Banbury wool market or in Chipping Campden. Most farms kept pigs primarily for meat, although the pigs were also useful in clearing poor land by their rooting action. Many householders kept pigs and a few remaining pigsties, now tidy brick sheds, can still be seen at the back of some of the Victorian houses, for example along the Warwick Road. 'Household' pigs continued to provide an important part of the diet well into the 20th century. Some households had two, one for family consumption and one for sale. One village trader, who supplied animal foodstuffs to augment the pigs' diet of household scraps, recalls that some very poor families would ask if they could pay their bill after they had sold the pig - and, he adds, this they did without fail, "very honestly and promptly".

On lighter land, seed crops were grown in rotation - wheat for flour and bran, barley for cattle meal, and oats for horses. Tall flax was grown for the widely-used linen fibre made from the straw, though its shorter relative, linseed, was never very successful on the wet soils of the Kineton area. Vetches and clover improved the land and were useful for seed and fodder; and

Kineton schoolchildren perform 'the Bean Setting Dance'

crops of potatoes cleared the ground and were the working man's staple diet. Field beans were also grown in large numbers on the lighter land in the area, and were a crop of considerable importance. Older varieties, sown in spring or autumn according to conditions, were a valuable addition to the protein content of animal feed, but more recently small spring sown 'tic beans' have been sold to the pigeon racing community in towns and cities, and have proved a surprisingly prolific and profitable crop. The records between 1844 and 1854 of the Lines family, who farmed Battle Farm, describe the setting of the annual price of beans at Kineton market every 5 February, at the St Paul's Day fair. At May-time the children of the village school danced 'the Bean Setting dance', which may have origins similar to 'Strip the Willow', another country dance. 'Stripping the willow' was one of the processes needed in the preparation of willow osiers such as those grown in Kineton off the Banbury road.

With the coming of the Industrial Revolution both the look of the landscape and the importance of agricultural labour started to change. Even though labour was plentiful and cheap, the invention of the reaper binder and traction steam engines meant more could be done with less labour, faster and more efficiently. Although the coming of the railway in many places meant that cattle no longer had to be driven to market, the rail journey to Banbury market was not easy, and livestock continued to be taken by road. But drovers were soon replaced by vehicles, and horses were gradually replaced by machinery, and had it not been for the presence of the Warwickshire Hunt kennels, all the trades associated with the care of horses would have been threatened.

The Shaping of a Community

The two World Wars accelerated the change. The First World War took horses away from the farms, and the Second compelled every farmer to plough as much grassland as possible and to cultivate arable and root crops. The government body responsible for the overall planning of wartime farming, the War Agricultural Executive Committee, colloquially known as the "War Ag", was empowered to enforce the changes they thought necessary. In the Kineton area, where land was heavy and fields poorly drained, the idea of changing from centuries of grassland to cereal farming met with a great deal of scepticism. The local farmers used their ingenuity in keeping fields as well drained as they could. One method involved ploughing the top of a ridge into a furrow one year, and then ploughing it out again, back into a sort of ridge and furrow, the next year. Others found they could grow the best crops by sowing their wheat into something resembling a field earthed up for potatoes. Rationing of food imposed on the civilian population even extended to the keeping of livestock. The villagers who kept pigs in their gardens were organised into 'Pig Clubs', and were allowed only a ration of barley meal and grain for their animals. The Kineton 'Pig Club' was set up by the War Ag, but its administration relied on the goodwill of local grain merchants. By the end of the war, horse power had given way to tractors. The success of the Women's Land Army had shown that farm traditions could change, and just as girls were drafted in from towns and cities to take the place of men on the farms, so people left the country for better paid jobs in industry. Hunting went into decline, motor vehicles became commonplace, farms became more mechanized and the need for labour dwindled. The coming of the combine harvester and hydraulics on tractors ended the great threshing machine

A reaper-binder

gangs. New sprays, seeds and fertilisers all brought higher yields. Many local farms turned from dairying and beef rearing to grow a wide range of arable crops, and employed contractors with the latest equipment to manage their farms.

In view of the heavy dependence on agriculture, it is not surprising that there is little evidence of the development in Kineton of trades unconnected with either the land or the needs of the population of a small town. Only after the 18th century do various trade directories and census forms give lists of the occupations of the inhabitants. These show how the more enterprising increasingly turned to a number of trades to make money and to improve their way of life generally. An indication of how the populace earned its living is given in the Earl of Warwick's 1774 survey. Among those listed are *John Clarke, a Flax Dresser* (preparing flax for the making of linen cloth), *John Sheler, a Wool Comber* (carding out the wool staple ready for spinning), *John Attrik, a Tallow Chandler* (making and selling tallow candles - the main form of lighting at this time), *Timothy Kilby, a Glover* (making and selling gloves), *Thomas Garrett, a Cordwainer* (making and selling shoes), *John Foster, an Apothecary* (making and selling medicines), and *John Gibbs, a Ploughwright* (making and repairing ploughs). Later directories continue to name entirely predictable occupations, including stonemasons, carpenters, sawyers and thatchers, needed for the building and furnishing of substantial houses and cottages made with the local stone from quarries at Edgehill and Hornton, or with bricks. Kineton had its own brickworks, which baked the characteristic yellow bricks seen in the older houses up the Warwick Road and in, for example, the Post Office on Banbury Street. The site of the brickworks was where the footpath across Big Field now meets the Red Road, but there is little to see but a few broken remains of the kilns. The only known manufacturing industry, the making of rough woollen hosiery, had died out by 1854.

Many tradespeople had several means of making money, and amongst others we find references in White's Directory of 1874 to *Martin Wisdom, Snr, Basketmaker and Fishmonger; Josiah Woodley, Maltster Seed and Hop Merchant and Insurance Agent; William Garrett, Parish Clerk and Cooper* (barrel maker). Not surprisingly, in a village that was largely self-sufficient, there were always numerous butchers, grocers and bakers. Cattle and sheep took up a large acreage of land around Kineton, and although many were taken to larger towns for sale, others were killed in Kineton. The slaughterman would very often travel around the area killing beasts. Joe Shepherd was a pig-killer at the turn of the century - happily combining this with his other job as Kineton's Town Crier! Pork products were sold at the pork butchers in Southam Street and in 1874 Kineton had three butchers, and Little Kineton one. There were also four bakers and no less than nine addresses for grocery and provision dealers, some of whom also sold wine. Although the number of shops was much reduced, in the late 1990s the village still had a butcher, greengrocer and general grocer, but the last baker closed in 1970.

Village men doing manual work, especially those working on the land, have understandably always had prodigious thirsts. To cater for this need, Kineton had several inns, and a few small premises where beer and ale were brewed. Rumour puts the number at 11, but certainly some six or seven are well documented. They include two which are still licensed, the Swan Inn, formerly the White Swan and Posting Hotel, and the Carpenters Arms in Banbury Street. The name of the Red Lion, a former coaching inn at the corner of Bridge Street, still exists as Red Lion House, but the Rose and Crown and the New Inn in Market Square, the Drum and Monkey at the bottom of Bridge Street, and the Woolpack Inn and the Railway Inn in Banbury Street have disappeared. At one time Kineton had its own part-time excise officer, William Woodley, to watch over all these establishments, and to collect the required excise duty in addition to his own work as a clock maker and repairer. Licences for the sale of beer and spirits were issued by Justices of the Peace sitting at Kineton.

Another main source of employment in Kineton was connected with horses. All through the ages, men have used horses for transport, work and pleasure. Kineton was no exception and for a long period much of its income was derived from hunting and various horse associated trades. In 1850, it is recorded that there were no fewer than five wheelwrights, three saddlers, three blacksmiths and three boot and shoe makers. When the Lords Willoughby de Broke became Masters of the Warwickshire Hunt, the importance of the trades connected with horses took on even greater significance. The building of the hunt kennels in Little Kineton in 1839 was the beginning of the golden days of village trade. The Warwickshire Hunt rapidly became one of the most fashionable packs in the country, and the visitors who came to ride to hounds brought with them many servants and wealth hitherto unknown to Kineton. All sorts of services were required, and in 1874, as a reflection of the times, a variety of genteel trades were being carried on in Kineton. These included *Charlotte Freeman, Southam Street*, dressmaker; *Mary Taylor, Southam Street*, milliner; and *Ann Wisdom, Banbury Street*, fancy repository. The hairdresser was *John Quartermaine*, and stationery could be bought from *John Coop* of Banbury Street. Six

Vic Wills and his cycle shop in Banbury Street

drapers served the needs of the village for linen and wool cloth, including the Co-operative Industrial and Provident Society in Manor Lane. There were also four tailors and drapers supplying and making up clothes. Transport by cab could be obtained from Thomas Wesson of Banbury Street, and Kineton's ironmonger, Thomas Griffin, was listed as *general furnishing and builder's ironmonger, oil and colour merchant and agricultural implement agent*. He traded from his shop in Warwick Road, on the site of what was to become the Midland Bank.

For a period, lighting in the houses and streets was provided by gas from the Kineton Gas Light, Coal and Coke Company in Warwick Road, and coal merchants operated from the station yard. To meet the demand for road transport and petrol, several garages were established. At least one was trading before 1912, and until the late 70s and 80s three garages serviced the village cars. Two are now closed, Percy Gilks in Banbury Road, and the Kineton Garage which was under the old Public Hall, but the Station Garage remains in business.

In this computerised age, when electronic contact can be made at the touch of a button, it is becoming possible to open offices in areas with low overheads, where a high quality of life is achievable. Kineton trade is thus in the process of change to this new style of working, and new design and publishing businesses are beginning to occupy the empty shops. As long as new people, whose basic needs are still the same as Kinetonians of old, come to live in the village, it seems likely that many of the old shops and services will survive.

Helping the Poor, the Needy and the Unemployed

Before the development of the Welfare State in the 20th century, the 'necessitous poor' of Kineton had to rely on help in adversity from two sources, the Overseers of the Poor and the gifts from charitable bequests. The main responsibility for the care of the poor, the sick and the elderly lay with members of the Parish Vestry, which consisted of the vicar, the two churchwardens and a number of other leading citizens who, in Kineton, were co-opted rather than elected. They administered the local charities and each year appointed from their number two men to serve as Overseers of the Poor. The quality of the provision depended very much on their enthusiasm (or lack of it), and, fortunately, in the 19th century at least, the people of Kineton appear to have benefited from a paternalistic and generally sympathetic approach. Some credit for this must go to William Johns, the village schoolmaster, who also served as churchwarden and parish clerk in the early years of that century and was tireless in his correspondence on behalf of the poor and unemployed.

The average amount needed to support the poor each year was £500, but unpredictable bad harvests and freezing weather could bring widespread seasonal unemployment in the countryside, and epidemics could cause sudden demands to be made on the medical services. Nevertheless, a recent study has shown that the percentage of Kineton's population receiving relief remained at a constant 5%, which was less than half the national average of 11%.

The Overseers of the Poor

The overseers, who received no payment for their work, raised revenue from local rates and had personal responsibility for deciding the merits of appeals for help. This help could take many forms. As well as regular weekly cash payments, the overseers gave practical assistance whenever possible. The poor were helped to find work, maybe as part of an arrangement whereby the daily rate of pay was agreed by the Vestry and the cost shared between the employer and the parish. Women might be provided with spinning wheels and yarn. Efforts were made to place young girls in employment within the village ; in 1809, Mr Bishop, a baker, took the youngest daughter of the late Elizabeth Clarke on the understanding that he would "find, provide and allow her sufficient meat, drink, lodging and washing for twelve months" in return for two shillings a week from the parish. If work could not be found locally, " healthy active girls, not under 4 feet 6 inches in height" might find themselves apprenticed in the cotton mills of Benjamin Smart near Warwick or even the Amber Cotton Factory in Derbyshire.

There was also some assistance with the cost of medical care. In 1812 the overseers supplied two surgeons with "a list of the paupers of this parish" and asked them to tender for the provision of "surgery medicines and attendance for one year". Mr Welchman agreed to "attend to the poor for one year for eight guineas, as usual", with the proviso that the parish "allow something extra should anything serious happen". The previous year the Parish Vestry spent a great deal of money by sending "a labouring man, a pauper of our parish in a deranged state of mind" to a surgeon in Henley-in-Arden for treatment.

Just as today, subsidies were given to help with heating costs. During the winter months coal would be supplied to the poor cheaply or even free of charge. George Lines, an overseer in 1854, reduced the charge on the rates by maintaining a "subscription list for the purpose of supplying the poor of Kineton with coals at 6d per hundredweight"; this was headed by Lord Willoughby de Broke with 10 tons and followed by forty others offering amounts from half-a-crown to two pounds in money.

Charities

At various times the Parish Vestry has had responsibility for administering at least seven charitable bequests. Over the years the smaller bequests were amalgamated to form larger charities, eventually being joined together with one from Combroke to form the Kineton United Charities.

In his will of 1660, Thomas Aylworth had bequeathed £200 to provide a dozen loaves of bread for distribution to the poor each Sunday and coats and gowns for two poor men and two poor women on St Thomas's Day, 21 December. By 1914 the number of gowns distributed to those "thought the most deserving" had risen to twenty-three and the coats to seven. In 1894, at the parish church, Ballard's Bread Charity distributed 132 four pound loaves to the poor of Kineton. By 1911 the distribution had moved to the Church Rooms and, in the words of the Stratford Herald, "The recipients were evidently pleased with the gift, as on the stroke of twelve the room was literally besieged. The three Kineton bakers each received a share of patronage."

Kineton's largest charitable bequest came from Josiah Woodley, who died in 1887 leaving £1000, the interest from which was to be "applied on New Year's Day for the benefit of the necessitous poor of Kineton. This handsome addition to the charities of the town is much appreciated by the inhabitants, as further proof of the kindly and generous character of their

Josiah Woodley with Fred Phillips on his knee, about 1860.

late respected neighbour." Unfortunately Josiah Woodley's death coincided with the spectacular failure of Greenway's Bank in Warwick and it took nearly five years for the Court of Chancery to release money to the trustees. In the early 1900s the charity was distributed in the form of tickets "for clothing, firing, or grocery" redeemable at the local shops, "the families receiving one for 2s 6d, others two for the same amount, while three were given to widows and deserving cases." In 1923 there were 92 recipients.

Since 1969 there have been only two local charities, the Bentley Charity for Apprenticing, and the Relief in Need Charity, administered together as the Kineton United Charities. The main thrust of the Bentley Charity is in assisting students under 25 with the purchase of books and equipment for further education at college or university. The Relief in Need Charity continues the centuries old tradition of "relieving either generally or individually persons who are in conditions of need, hardship or distress" by making grants of money, or helping in other appropriate ways.

The Shaping of a Community

Schools in Kineton

Although a 'Free School' had been founded in neighbouring Combroke by Sir Grevill Verney of Compton Verney in 1641, the earliest reference we can find to a school in Kineton is in 1662, when Peter Bishop was licensed "to teach school". During the 19th century schools became more numerous and varied, and were increasingly able to meet the needs and ambitions of all levels of society. At the end of the 20th century only two schools remain, but each serves an area much larger than the parish of Kineton itself.

The 'Village Schools'
The National School, circa 1811-1884

Throughout the 19th century popular education for boys and girls was provided at the 'village' school, which became known as the 'National' school when, in 1819, it affiliated to the National Society for the Education of the Poor according to the Principles of the Church of England. At this time the schoolroom was in Southam Street, where William Johns had been running a school for children of the poor for several years. A Parish Vestry meeting in 1820 agreed

> All paupers of this parish that have children that can go to school and are admitted by the School Committee, if they do not attend school regularly, to be taken off 3d a day for every day absent unless leave is asked of the Master.

The school was supported by subscriptions and run as both a Day and a Sunday School; and a government survey of 1833 records that 35 boys and 42 girls were attending on weekdays, whilst 47 boys and 45 girls attended on Sunday.

Then, in 1840, the school moved to a new building in the centre of the Market Place, erected through the generosity of Lord Willoughby de Broke on the site of the old market house. The following year, at the age of 23, Caroline Randall took over the school from William Johns. She soon married a village carpenter and, as Mrs Caroline Blunt, taught in three separate school buildings for over fifty years before retiring at the age of 72.

When the building in the centre of the Market Square became too small, the vicar, the Rev Francis Miller, had a new school built on Southam Street and took close managerial control of its running until his death in 1890. Initially Caroline Blunt remained in charge, but the 1870 Elementary Education Act brought her a succession of male colleagues to whom she gradually lost overall responsibility. This change was not without its tensions; in 1872 the Master, George Tucker, recorded in the school log book

> Whilst punishing (and only moderately) Edward Dickinson for gross insubordination, the Mistress interfered and took his part and sent for the Vicar who came and ordered **before all the children** that there should be no punishment inflicted only by the mistress.

Although the Rev Mr Miller was clearly a compassionate man - George Tucker was described as "a cripple from infancy" - he did not always make successful appointments. There was a particularly bad period in 1876-77 when one master resigned after arguments over discipline, a second gave up after only seven months "in consequence of unfitness for a [teaching] certificate through a paralytic affection of his side" and a third "gave up his situation of his own choice" after only a month's service. Long-term stability came in 1884 with the appointment of Joseph Chandler, who continued as headmaster for over thirty nine years and taught several of the people still living in Kineton today. His long service made a welcome change, for prior to his coming there had been seven masters in twelve years.

Joseph Chandler, headmaster for 39 years.

From National to Primary School 1884-1957

It was Joseph Chandler who had to respond to increasingly severe criticism from Her Majesty's Inspectors of the inadequacies of the building in Southam Street, and to rise above the local political conflict when a School Board was proposed. It was he who supervised the move in 1892 across the Market Square to yet another new building on a site by the church, and he who dealt with the transfer of the school to Warwickshire County Council control as a church school in 1903. When he retired in 1924, this exceptional headmaster had seen the school leaving age rise from 11 to 14 and provision made for "the sharpest children" to continue their education up to 16 outside Kineton at Central Schools in Wellesbourne, Tysoe and Stratford.

Following the 1936 Education Act, which required that all children above the age of 11 should be educated in a Senior School, active consideration was given to the building of such a school in Kineton. Most energetic in support and promotion of the idea was the Honourable Mabel Verney, who died in 1937, before the plan could become reality. The outbreak of the Second World War further postponed educational decisions, and when finally approved, the post-war educational development plan for Warwickshire provided a new non-denominational secondary school for Kineton and the neighbouring villages and a new church primary school for the younger children from a smaller area. But for that, and other huge changes brought about by the war, it is possible that Kineton would now have a 'Mabel Verney Church of England Senior School' as well as its Church of England Primary School.

Kineton High School and Kineton C.E. Primary School from 1957

When Kineton High School opened on the Banbury Road in September 1957 there were 270 pupils and a staff of twelve; by 1961 numbers had risen to over 400 children and 25 teachers. The original buildings were intended for 360 pupils, and comprised a hall, a library, eleven classrooms and four practical rooms for woodwork, housecraft, science and art. Continued expansion has seen the school providing secondary education for well over 1,000 young people aged 11-18 from an area which stretches from Ettington to Fenny Compton.

It was not until 1970 that the 7-11 year-old children could transfer from the 1892 building on the Market Square to the new primary school building on land off King John's Road, and the old building with its lofty schoolroom and outside toilets was not vacated altogether by the youngest children until 1990.

Some Other Schools

For some years after the transfer of the National School to the Market Square premises in 1840, William Johns' daughter, Alice, continued to run her own day and boarding school in Southam Street.

A Mathematical and Commercial Academy was opened by J Selmin Brewer on the Warwick Road in 1848 and was the subject of a typically self-confident notice in the Warwick Advertiser declaring

> In the above Establishment, Young Gentlemen are genteelly Boarded and expeditiously Educated for Five Pounds per Quarter. Extras carefully avoided. The pupils are instructed in the English, Latin, and in every branch of polite and useful Literature; the Greek and French Languages by Qualified Masters, if required. The Premises, including an extensive Play-ground, a large and airy School-room, recently erected, and fitted up in the most convenient manner, are particularly healthy; the provisions are of the best quality, and without limitation at any meal. The Pupils are treated with parental kindness. Parents who wish to have their Sons carefully and expeditiously educated either for Professional, Commercial, or Agricultural pursuits, would find Mr Brewer's system of Education efficient and economical.

A few years later James Winger was running a similar 'commercial academy' in Bridge Street, apparently with some success, for in 1858, when Kineton was celebrating the election of Colonel Cartwright as Member of Parliament

> children of the National School and pupils of Mr Winger's academy, numbering together about 170, were regaled with a substantial dinner in one of the marquees.

At about the same time the 'Kineton Ladies School' was operating in Banbury Street. The principal, Miss Barbara Edmunds, was thanking her friends for "the liberal patronage already bestowed upon her"; and also assuring them that her "utmost endeavours will be exerted for the moral and intellectual improvement" of her pupils.

Diana Lodge, Little Kineton

Kineton Lodge School

Diana Lodge **[E8]**, on the edge of the green in Little Kineton, was once known as Kineton Lodge School. This flourished between the late 1850s and 1883 as a 'classical school' (an early form of preparatory school) for young boys from upper middle class homes. The headmaster throughout this period was James Hunter, who was over 70 years of age when the school closed. In December 1857 the innkeeper at the Swan felt able to charge fourteen shillings for each journey conveying the "young gentlemen from Mr. Hunter's school" to Banbury or Leamington in his Whitechapel cart - rather more than his normal fare! The young Bolton King from nearby Chadshunt Hall attended the school for four years, before entering Eton in 1872 at the age of 12. Other pupils of note included Sir Henry Palk Carew, an eleven-year-old baronet related to the Willoughby de Brokes, and also two brothers, Edward and Ernest Knight, who could claim Jane Austen, author of *Pride and Prejudice,* as their great-great-aunt.

Kineton Middle Class School

The school premises on the Warwick Road were erected by Georgiana Lady Willoughby de Broke in 1862 at a time when, according to her daughter the Honourable Mabel Verney, 'middle class education was deficient in the country'. It would, however, appear that a school was already operating under this name in Kineton as a replacement for the old Grammar School in Combroke. George Edward Dodson, the first headmaster, was able to receive boarders in the New School House on 13 April 1863, "offering moderate terms for both boarders and day pupils". In later years the school could accommodate up to 30 boarders and all pupils were offered a playground of 15 acres. The school is now best remembered as 'Webb's School', after its last principal, Guernsey Walsingham Webb. He was appointed in 1889 at the age of 24, having previously run a boys school in Bridge Street. At his new school he offered a "sound commercial education, including Shorthand and Book-keeping, and a good ground work in Classics and Mathematics" in a "healthy locality". In 1905 he was joined by his sister, who moved her school for 'young ladies' from Bridge Street to Warwick Road. The school closed in the early 1920s, soon after Mr Webb entered holy orders at the age of 56.

Littledale and Manor Lane Schools

Private fee-paying education continued to be available in Kineton for young children until after the Second World War. Littledale School on the Lighthorne Road could count two future Lords Lieutenant and the boy who would train three Grand National winners among its pupils in the late 1930s. Manor Lane School was started in the Old Estate Cottage in Manor Lane and was transferred to the larger premises of Clarendon House in Bridge Street in 1954.

Fire Services

Kineton has a proud tradition of fire-fighting service that can be traced back to the early 19th century. Since then the people of Kineton have found the presence of a fire engine in their midst reassuring and have responded readily when help or money were needed. The newspaper reports on which this brief history is based have recorded a slow progress from manual pump to motorised transport, and have not hesitated to comment when the enthusiasm or efficiency of the voluntary fire fighters has been in doubt.

Early in 1822 money had been raised in the parish for the purchase of "a Fire Ingeon, Ladders, Fire Hooks, etc", with five pounds subscribed by the local insurance agent of the County Fire Office. This equipment was kept in the chancel of the parish church, and fire fighters were summoned by the ringing of a church bell. For the next sixty years newspapers carried an occasional report of the engine in action, such as that for March 1857, when a fire broke out on a farm about a mile from Kineton.

> An alarm being given in the town, the inhabitants in great numbers repaired to the spot, when a stack of stubble, a straw rick, and clover rick, were found to be in flames. The Kineton fire-engine was promptly in attendance, and the exertions of all persons present, with the assistance of the engine, were directed to saving the barn.

Kineton: The Village and its History

The engine from the Compton Verney estate came to Kineton's assistance in December 1878, and helped save several ricks when a barn at Walton Farm on the Banbury Road was destroyed in a severe fire. In the same week, the people of Stratford-upon-Avon followed the example of such towns as Kenilworth, Nuneaton and Banbury by agreeing to set up a Volunteer Fire Brigade like the one which had been successful in Coventry for some fifteen years. It was not until June 1884 that the idea of a Volunteer Fire Brigade was taken up, and it was reported that

> the town of Kineton has this week been supplied with another fire engine on a much larger scale than the old one, which is very small and worn out. The fresh engine has been in use at Hereford and, we understand, is a very good one.

The Fire Brigade in the Market Square, 1931

The man entrusted with the purchase was Joseph Carter, road surveyor, of Pittern Hill Villa, who offered to serve as captain "if a team could be established to man the engine". Even then, it must have taken some time to recruit the first brigade "of very respectable and able-bodied young men", for it was not until March of the following year that they met at the Red Lion Hotel "for the purpose of trying on their helmets". In the June, 1885, sixteen men assembled for drill

> they were all fairly punctual, and they marched from the Red Lion to the engine house in the Market Square, when they soon had the two engines out, and ran them down to the brook, where some good practice was gone through, and each one performed his part exceedingly well for beginners.

After enjoying an immunity from fires for a long period, in 1887 the Kineton Brigade was called to two within a week, and its apparently poor performance provoked severe criticism. Following the first fire, the Stratford Herald commented

> About two years ago, when new appliances were obtained, a great deal was said as to the state of efficiency to which the brigade would be worked up. Numerous drills took place, and proper uniform was provided for the members. But, like a new toy to a child, interest in the engine soon began to flag.

A week later the same newspaper reported

> Both the Kineton engines were hurried to the scene, but they proved of little service. In consequence of their inefficient condition a delay of an hour and a half to two hours was created before they could be put in operation, and even then their performance was of a poor description. At the expiration of that time, the largest engine was got to work a little, but so feebly that, it is said, it would not put out a piece of lighted paper. The smaller engine appeared the better of the two, for considerably less time was necessary to get that into working order. After two such narrow escapes we should think that the residents of Kineton will insist upon something being done to place themselves in a safer condition. The present discreditable state of affairs has existed long enough.

There were problems of a different kind in January 1890 when the brigade was summoned to another rick fire.

> Soon after the discovery was made the alarm bell was rung at the church, which soon summoned the fire brigade, most of whom turned out, but some little delay was caused, as the key to the engine-house was not kept close at hand. Nothing daunted, the door was soon broken open, and the engine was run up to the scene of the fire, and got to work as quickly as possible.

This time the problems were addressed more effectively. Within a week, a meeting of the members of the fire brigade and representatives of two fire insurance offices had been held, and remedial action agreed, including a notice on the engine house door indicating where the keys were kept. By June the Stratford Herald was more optimistic.

> The newly-constructed brigade mustered at the engine-house on Thursday evening, under the command of Captain John Brown and Vice-Captain W E Coles, when the hose and other appliances were thoroughly inspected and tested, and found to be in fair working order. A drill took place upon the Warwick-road. The water for the purpose was procured from one of the hydrants of the newly laid mains from the waterworks. A trial was also made with a hose attached to a stand pipe, which answered admirably, the pressure upon the water being found sufficient to send it well over the highest house in the place.

W E Coles took over as captain at the end of 1890 and continued until his retirement in 1939.

The Fire Brigade about 1950

A new engine, painted vermilion with the name *KINETON* in gilt and shaded letters on each side, was obtained from Messrs Shand, Mason, and Co, of Blackfriars, London, in 1892.

> It is fitted with suck pumps, and at its highest speed will deliver water at the rate of one hundred gallons per minute and a jet of 120 feet in height. It is of a size to be worked by 22 men, and has carrying accommodation for eight men besides the driver.

The working of this manual machine proved expensive and as Kineton's tradesmen replaced their horses with motor vehicles, so it became increasingly difficult for the fire service to find the horses they needed in an emergency. There are alarming stories of the delays whilst horses were brought from a farm in Butlers Marston. The purchase of a motor fire engine was considered in 1924, but it was not until 1931 that a second-hand Dennis motor appliance was acquired from the Guildford Fire Service.

The volunteer fire brigade remained outside local authority control until 1948, when responsibility for the service was transferred to Warwickshire County Council. A new fire station was opened on the Warwick Road in 1955, replacing the one in the Market Place, which had been in use since 1885. Then, some forty years later, following the rapid expansion of neighbouring Wellesbourne, came the proposal to provide cover from a newly built fire station there and to close the Kineton station in 1999. This would be a sad end to an institution that has served Kineton and its surroundings so well and for so many years.

The Shaping of a Community

Kineton's Own Gas Company

Although Kineton is no longer supplied with gas from the mains, it once had its own gas company. A public meeting "to consider the propriety of forming a company to supply the town of Kineton with gas" was held at the Swan Inn on 6 February 1863. At that meeting, Mr T A Hedley, a consulting engineer from Banbury, who had been employed in similar undertakings in Banbury, Southam, Shipston-on-Stour, and Henley-in-Arden, explained the working of the system in those towns and expressed the view that

> if a company were formed it would not only be of great advantage to the inhabitants, but also yield an adequate return to the shareholders.

The total outlay required for the purchase of a suitable site on the Warwick Road, erection of works, and all incidental expenses, was estimated to be about £1,500. By the end of the meeting it was agreed that 'The Kineton Gas-light, Coal and Coke Company' should be formed with a capital of £1,500 in 750 shares of £2 each, and half those shares had already been taken up.

Four days later, on 10 February, the company was registered under the provisions of the Company's Act 1862, and the remaining shares advertised in the local press. The nine provisional

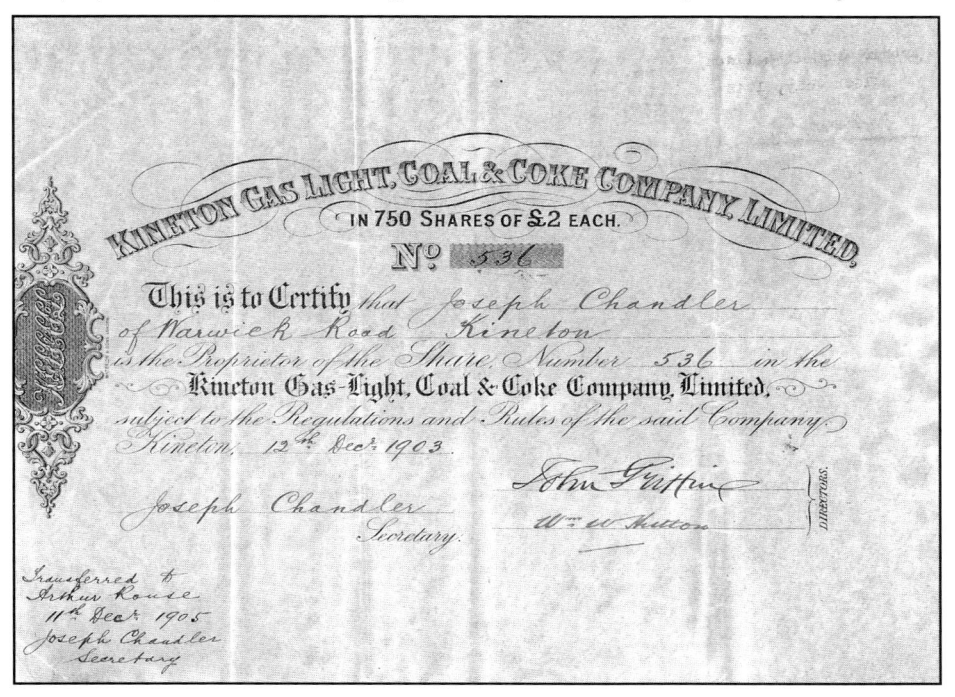

A share certificate issued to Joseph Chandler, village schoolmaster and Gas Company Secretary.

directors, listed in the advertisement as auctioneer, baker, draper, grocer, innkeeper, ironmonger, plumber, saddler and surgeon, all lived and worked in Kineton. Under their direction, the contract with Messrs Porter & Co. of Lincoln for the erection of the works was signed on 26 May. Less than six months later, on 2 November, the new works were opened and the gas entered the mains.

At the start of trading in November 1863, the works included a gasholder with a capacity of 4,000 cubic feet and

> more than 500 lights had been taken, Colonel Cartwright [a Northamptonshire M.P. living in Little Kineton] and Colonel North [Master of the Warwickshire Hunt] being amongst the customers.

Affairs appear to have progressed well and, although some adjustments were required to the manufacturing process, company dividends rose from 4% at the outset to 5% by 1866.

A significant enlargement of the works occurred during 1868-69, when Lord Willoughby de Broke put up a proposition for supplying his mansion, farm buildings and workshops at Compton Verney with gas, and the supply was also taken to Combroke. As a result, there were now two gasholders capable between them of containing 12,000 cubic feet, and the share capital was increased to £2,300. The cost of the expansion, however, considerably exceeded the original estimate and the directors felt unable to declare a dividend in 1869. Fortunately for the shareholders this unhappy state of affairs did not last long and by 1880 the company was paying them a dividend of 10%.

In 1885 'The Gas Question' hit the headlines when William Wilson, the headmaster of the Middle School across the road from the gasworks, organised a public meeting chaired by Lord

The Gas Works. The entrance to Little Pittern has now replaced the retort house.

Willoughby de Broke. Mr Wilson alleged inaccurate meter reading and over-charging by a senior official and director of the company. This attack on the integrity of a fellow resident of Kineton did not go unchallenged. Six months later Mr Wilson had emigrated to New Zealand.

The enterprising local company became involved with two significant projects during 1889, one to improve Kineton's water supply, the other to provide street lighting. By the late 1880s Kineton's water supply system was totally inadequate and the directors of the gas company were asked by the local authority to form a company to take it over. Although Lord Willoughby de Broke had offered to present them with the tanks and existing apparatus, the directors, "in consequence of so few requiring the water, did not consider the income would be sufficient to pay the shareholders a remunerative dividend" and turned down the request. Towards the end of the year they were more helpful, and agreed to participate in a scheme to provide and maintain street lights at a fixed charge of one pound per lamp, to be funded by public subscription. Twenty-two lamps were erected and they were maintained by public subscription well into the 20th century, although during some winters they were not lit due to lack of funds.

As a local concern, the Kineton Gas-light, Coal and Coke Company attracted loyal service from many of the residents. Josiah Woodley, auctioneer, was chairman from 1863 until his death in 1887, and was followed by John Griffin, grocer, until his death in 1915. Secretaries to the board included George Lines, assistant overseer and rate collector, Joseph Chandler, headmaster of the Church School, and George Orme Tiley, scoutmaster and private secretary to Lord Willoughby de Broke. Directors continued to be local men and resigned when they left Kineton.

With the coming of electricity in the 1930s, the fortunes of the gas company declined and residents often felt that they could tell the moods of the father and son managing the works from the considerable fluctuations in the quality of heat and light they received. It was not, however, an easy life producing gas; back in 1911 the manager's nineteen year old son died, having been enveloped in steam and terribly scalded whilst clearing the clinker from the firehole. The company carried on until after the Second World War, but a liquidator was appointed in 1948, and it was finally dissolved on 19 April 1951. There is at least one disconnected gas meter still lurking in a Kineton cellar to this day.

Kineton's Mills

Near the top of Pittern Hill, at the side of the road to Wellesbourne, is a stone windmill tower. This is the last survivor of a number of windmills that have served the village and its immediate neighbourhood over the last seven hundred years. In *Warwickshire Windmills*, published by the County Museum in 1979, W A Seaby records details of five earlier windmills and whereas some of these were simply replacements of earlier structures, it is likely that for many centuries the parish had at least two working mills. Seaby records two 'Manor' windmills, each built by 1279 and recorded again in 1325, and a further two mills built by 1565. There is no evidence of the location of these early mills, but a fifth mill, built by 1725, is described as being 1 mile WNW of the church, on high ground to the north of the village, close to the boundary with Combroke parish and near to some early farm buildings on what is now known as Cow Common Farm. In fact the high ground surrounding Cow Common Farm, an area now called Pittern Hill, is the only part of the parish which is likely to have been a suitable site for a windmill.

A printed map, published in 1789, shows two windmills on Pittern Hill. The surviving structure - a barrel-like 'tower' mill, as distinct from the earlier wooden 'post' mills - is the more easterly. When offered for sale in 1808 the advertisement described it as a

> capital Stone Windmill, containing two pair of stones; together with Two Closes or Inclosed Grounds adjoining the same, situate, standing, lying, and being within the Parish of Great Kington aforesaid, in a place there, commonly called or known by the name of Windmill Hill Quarter; containing by estimation Nineteen Acres or thereabouts (more or less) now in the occupation of Mr William Bloxham.

The tower that we see today was built mainly of stone (now much patched), was lined internally with brick, and has three intermediate floors. The roof is not original, but is built on the original beams which would have carried the cap, windshaft and sails. The mill would have carried two pairs of mill-stones but sadly little of the original works remain, save some evidence of the way in which the cap would have turned to face the massive sails into the wind. After the end of its working life as a mill, it has been used to hold water storage tanks and as an observation post during the Second World War. The walls, floors and roof were restored with the assistance of Manpower Services Commission funds in 1985/7.

The remains of the windmill on Pittern Hill.

The decline of the windmill coincides with the erection of a steam corn mill at the other end of Kineton in Mill Lane, although it is likely that they co-existed for some years. In 1848 John Coles, baker, John Enock, gentleman, and John Griffin, saddler, jointly leased a large piece of what was then known as Dodds Green. By 1855 John Griffin had become the sole leaseholder and there was a

> Hot Steam Corn Mill with the Steam Engine, fixtures and implements there unto belonging, lately erected and built and now standing on the said piece of ground.

In January 1858 Mr Griffin advertised "A Steam Corn Mill, doing a good business, to be sold or let." The mill was then acquired by J F Smith, whose name is also associated with the Pittern Hill windmill and the farm at the corner of the Market Square. In the following December another advertisement appeared requesting

> all persons having any sacks marked 'Enoch, Coles, and Griffin' belonging to the above mill to forward them to the said J F Smith without delay.

Seven years later the Warwick Advertiser carried the following report of a serious accident.

> Mr J F Smith, of the steam flour mills, Kineton, was at work among the machinery, which was in motion at the time, when his foot slipped, and, before he could recover himself, he was struck by the fly-wheel of the engine, the splinter bone of his leg being fractured and his ankle dislocated. He was immediately attended by Doctor Fyfe, of Kineton, under whose care we are glad to hear he is going on favourably.

As farming became depressed at the end of the 19th century, and corn growing declined, milling ceased for a time. However, in 1900, the mill was purchased by Arthur Rouse and W E Coles who feared that it might otherwise be acquired by a brewery and thus adversely affect the trade in beer at their grocery store in Banbury Street **[B2]**. Arthur Rouse gradually built up a business supplying animal feed to local farmers and members of the hunting fraternity and he installed his own rolling and grinding mills and dressing machinery. Despite the decline in demand for horse feeds, the business, by then under the ownership of Arthur Rouse's grandson, Arthur Wheildon, continued at the mill until 1968.

The Railway

In 1851 Kineton's nearest railway station was 12 miles away, just as it is today. A year later, with the opening of a station at Harbury, the distance was halved. It was a further 19 years before Kineton had its own station, which, for a time, lay at one end of a developing branch line. The line linked Kineton to Fenny Compton, from where it was possible to take a train directly to London.

Proposals that would join Kineton to the national rail network had been made for several years, but it was only with the East and West Junction Railway Act of 1864 that Kineton was

Gangers working on the line at Kineton Station.

offered the real prospect of a through route. The primary aim of the promoters was to open up a direct route for the transport of iron ore from Northamptonshire to the steel mills of South Wales. The tradesmen of Kineton were, however, convinced of "the great advantages that must accrue to the town and neighbourhood" and the directors of Kineton's gas company were in no doubt that, as the station would be near the gas works, the line would "materially diminish the expenditure in the article of coal, and also tend to increase the consumption of gas."

As so often in 19th century railway history, ambition largely exceeded achievement, and lack of money meant that the scheme could be put in hand only in stages. Kineton was fortunate to be included as a terminus of the first section. Progress was not smooth. After a small portion of the embankment had been constructed at Fenny Compton, the work was suspended, litigation in Chancery ensued and it was generally understood that the projected line would be abandoned. Difficulties were resolved and late in 1870 the project re-emerged. The 1871 census returns for Kineton reveal a population increase of 200, which has been attributed to the presence of gangs of navvies engaged in building the railway. Despite delays caused by frequent earth slips in the deep cutting at Kineton, the death of a young man crushed under his wagon while working on the embankment, and a fire that damaged an engine and destroyed the Kineton engine shed, the line at last opened on 1 June 1871.

In its report of the opening the Warwick Advertiser describes the passenger station as

> a handsome brick and stone building, with convenient waiting rooms

The Shaping of a Community

and points out that

> a large quantity of coal has been brought to the Kineton Station, this important article having been previously carted from Stratford-on-Avon or Warwick, which of course added materially to the cost. The station at Kineton will, there is no doubt, be a large depot for coal, corn, and agricultural produce generally and prove a great advantage to the town.

Passengers taking the first train from Kineton at 7.05 am and changing at Fenny Compton could spend six hours in London and arrive back in Kineton at 8.45 pm.

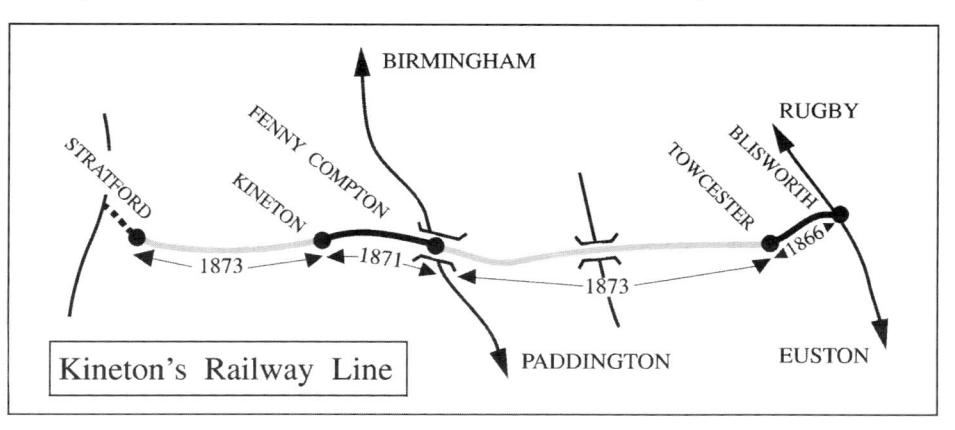

```
                    ▲ BIRMINGHAM
                                                    RUGBY
  STRATFORD   FENNY COMPTON      TOWCESTER  BLISWORTH
       KINETON
        ●———1873——●—1871—●           ●——1866—▶
                        ◀———1873——
  Kineton's Railway Line      ▼ PADDINGTON    ▼ EUSTON
```

Two years later the line was fully opened, with eastward extensions to Blisworth on the Euston to Birmingham mainline, and a westward extension to Stratford-upon-Avon. The official opening of the line was a gala occasion as much in Kineton as in Stratford.

> There were great rejoicings at Kineton. The station was nicely decorated with flags, and a special train, with the directors of the company, the principal landowners in the neighbourhood, the officials, and a number of friends, ran from Blisworth to Stratford, and afterwards returned to Kineton, where they had luncheon. In the evening the officials of the company had a dinner.

These rejoicings were short-lived, for in 1877 passenger services between Blisworth and Stratford were suspended. Until it became possible to reinstate a full service in 1885, only goods trains ran. On the resumption of passenger services the first train down was used by Lord Willoughby de Broke and the Warwickshire Hunt to transport their horses and hounds to a meet near Alcester, and for many years several horse boxes and a hound wagon were kept at Kineton Station for the Hunt. Nevertheless, partly because of a lack of enthusiasm among the major railway companies - like the Great Western and the Great Central lines in the Midlands - to use other companies' track, the line continued to face financial difficulties. In 1909 it was absorbed with others into the Stratford and Midland Junction Railway - the SMJ. In Kineton

Kineton: The Village and its History

Richard Greville Verney, 19th Lord Willoughby de Broke.

the change may have been barely noticeable, except for the opportunity for a new nickname - the 'Slow Miserable Journey' or even 'Slow Miserable and Jolty' Railway.

Lord Willoughby de Broke's heir took up his father's support for the line, and became a director of the new company. Each year from 1911 to 1914 he invited the company's entire staff to a party at Compton Verney, special trains bringing 250 people from both ends of the line to Kineton. He used the railway frequently for his journeys to the continent and for the two hour journey to London, having his meals served in his compartment in transit. Once, anxious to catch his connection, with the train already late, he tipped the guard at Kineton to ensure the time was made up. Unfortunately the driver saw; and continued on his slow way, stopping as scheduled for a horse box. The connection was missed. When his lordship remonstrated, the driver replied, "My lord, you greased the wrong end of the train!"

The line became part of the London Midland and Scottish in 1923, and during the Second World War gave vital service in transporting goods, both civilian and military. After the war, as railways generally became less used, Kineton also suffered. Passenger services between Blisworth and Stratford were withdrawn in 1952, and goods facilities in 1963. Following the complete closure of the line in 1965, all that remains in use is a four mile stretch from Fenny Compton to DM, Kineton. It came under army control in 1971 and links with the Army's internal rail system of 42 track miles.

Kineton was a railway town for less than a century. "Small time, but in that small most greatly lived." Not "this star of England" exactly, but a small and distinguished little station on a railway that meant much to those it served.

The Kineton Green Bus Service

The bus services from the village have had a colourful history - Kineton Green, Stratford Blue, Midland Red. More recently, after a period with David Grasby, the services were provided by Stagecoach.

The origins of the Kineton Green Bus Services Ltd are not to be found in Kineton but in nearby Bishops Itchington. In 1922 Charles Hunt started with one 14-seater bus and opened two routes from Bishops Itchington, one to Leamington and the other to Stratford. The venture was a success and two years later he moved to Kineton and with a second bus started regular services from here to Stratford and Leamington. At first the 14-seater was garaged at the corner of the Market Square opposite the Methodist Chapel, but later the buses were moved to premises near the railway station. As the business expanded the number of buses was increased, finally reaching six, and the 14-seaters were replaced by 20-seater and later 32-seaters.

The timetable for July 1933 shows seven services in operation:
> two to Banbury (one via Avon Dassett, the other via Fenny Compton)
> two to Leamington (one via Gaydon, the other via Moreton Morrell)
> two to Stratford (one via Ettington, the other via Moreton Morrell)
> and a short run to Radway

In addition to these regular services, the buses were available for private hire. Reports of outings and away matches regularly pay tribute to the helpfulness of Mr Hunt and his team.

A Kineton Green bus and its crew.

The experiences of the staff are also recalled with good humour, such as being given a piece of material to buy matching cotton in Leamington, or collecting or delivering parcels and letters (3d a letter, 6d a parcel). The summer uniform for female staff was a dress of green cotton, while the winter uniform included bottle green breeches, laced brown boots, greatcoat and a cap. On foggy nights a conductress might find herself walking in front of the bus with a white handkerchief tucked in the back of her belt.

Tragedy struck the Hunt family at least twice in the fourteen year history of the Kineton Green Service. In January 1930 Edna, Charles Hunt's 15 year old daughter, was killed when a Kineton Green bus collided with a lorry near Henley-in-Arden. Four years later, in the early hours of 10 September 1934, fire destroyed the whole fleet of five buses inside the recently built garage by the railway station. Nevertheless, by 8.15 am that day the usual services were running "with only 15 minutes delay" using buses hired from the Stratford Blue Company. Buses were later hired from the Red and White Company in Chepstow, and it was rumoured that a bus was seen some time later in Hereford still carrying details of Kineton Green fares.

On Friday 1 January 1937 the services operated by Kineton Green were taken over by Stratford-upon-Avon Blue Motors. Charles Hunt became landlord of the White Horse Hotel in Banbury and at a farewell dinner it was stated "He will be greatly missed in Kineton, where he took a big part in the life of the town, and where his business acumen was of great service. His interests were wide and generous."

The Warwickshire Hunt

The origins of the Warwickshire Hunt can be traced back to the arrival in 1795 of Mr John Corbet. Until then Warwickshire had been hunted only by small private packs of hounds, but Corbet had a greater vision, and for nearly twenty years hunted the whole county at his own expense. His generosity and enthusiasm were much missed when he left the area in 1821. It immediately became necessary to put the hunt on sound footings, by raising a subscription and building kennels, initially at Butlers Marston. The Warwickshire Hunt Club was established some five years later, in November 1826. Rule 9 of the newly formed Club stated

> The uniform of the Club for all the members not clergymen shall be a plain scarlet coat with gilt buttons, having on them an old English W.

After fifteen rent-free years at Butlers Marston, dues were suddenly demanded, and to avoid them the hounds were moved back to Stratford without delay.

When Mr Robert J. Barnard, later 17th Lord Willoughby de Broke, became Master in 1839 it was decided that kennels should be built on a site at Little Kineton. The land was given by Mr George Lucy of Charlecote, and Mr Hugh Williams, Lord Willoughby's agent, was appointed as architect. No fewer than 180 farmers brought over 550 wagon loads of materials to the site before building work started on 27 July and the kennels were occupied by 19 October, less than three months later. The development consisted of two houses, rooms for kennel servants, stabling for 23 horses, five kennels and feeding rooms. The total cost of this enterprise amounted

The Warwickshire Hunt meet in Little Kineton.

to £3,164 10s 6d - no small sum in those days. After the opening of the kennels, trade increased greatly in Kineton, with many of the gentry coming to the village and taking stables and lodges for the season. It was said that, at peak times, a stable was rented for fourteen shillings a week but a cottage for only ten shillings.

In 1877 the 18th Baron Lord Willoughby de Broke became Master of the Hunt. Under his direction the Warwickshire hounds became renowned for their excellent breeding, and for several years took many of the best trophies at the famous Peterborough Hound Show. By 1887 the eighty couples were all black, white and tan, this unusual triple colour being due entirely to the personal preference and enthusiasm of the Master. Around this time the annual Warwickshire Hunt Puppy Show was established and it became the custom to combine this with lunch in the grounds of nearby Kineton House.

The first Warwickshire Hunt Point-to-Point was held in 1832 with a course stretching from a point near Oakley Wood to Chesterton Windmill. It was laid down that "no rider was to open a gate, pass over a bridge or take a road." These races were held intermittently, at different locations. On 9 April 1892 the annual Parliamentary Point-to-Point Race and the Midland Sportsmen's Race were both held at Herd Hill, on the road to Oxhill. Over 300 people attended, including Members of the House of Commons who travelled to Kineton by special train from London. The M.P.s for Totnes and East Wilts won their respective weight class, but the Midland Sportsmen's Race was the climax. It included Captain W G 'Bay' Middleton, the Scottish companion of Elizabeth, Empress of Austria. He had apparently told a friend that this would be his last race. His premonition proved only too accurate for whilst jumping a simple fence he had a fatal fall into the Graveyard Field - site of the coppice where many of those who fell at Edgehill are believed to be buried. A memorial to the Captain was placed in the field, but it is now within the bounds of the Ammunition Depot and cannot be visited.

Later in 1892 the Warwickshire held its first Horse Show in Kineton, and these shows became a feature of the Hunt Calendar for many years. They were for horses belonging to farmers residing in the Warwickshire country and were started to encourage tenant farmers to breed "the two most useful kinds of horses they possibly can - cart horses and weight-carrying hunters". Hunter mares, thought the organisers, were "able to do a considerable amount in the field and in the cart, and earn their keep when they are in foal."

Hunting was badly disrupted by World War I. Kennel staff volunteered or were called up and a great number of horses were commandeered and sent overseas, many never to return. Even so, from 1911 to 1924 under Joint Masters Lord Willoughby de Broke and Mr Joshua Fielden, the Hunt had a sound basis. Joshua Fielden lived for hunting and was described as "very cool, has a fine eye for a country, and knows all the time what the hounds are doing".

In the 1930s there was still stabling for 400 horses in the Kineton area. The importance of the Warwickshire Hunt to Kineton between the Wars was summed up at a District Council debate in 1936.

> Kineton is unique. It is the centre of the Warwickshire Hunt; the Kennels are there: also many large residences, and there are more people of wealth at Kineton than in other village in the county. The Warwickshire Hunt seems to be booming. We have the best farms and the best huntsmen, and I am told that all the stables, garages, and houses are let. Hunting is the industry of Kineton. Anyone with a knowledge of hunting knows that each family brings about ten horses, two motor-cars, and a staff of servants. We want to encourage the hunting folk, who spend money and make a lot of difference to us.

Certainly many would argue that the Hunt was at its zenith during this period. It was one of the most fashionable places to be seen, and during this time many notable figures hunted with the Warwickshire. They included the then Prince of Wales, later the Duke of Windsor, and members of the Profumo family from Avon Dassett.

As in the First World War, hunting was on a reduced scale during the Second. Since then the Warwickshire Hunt has continued to thrive, although not on the scale of the thirties. It is still based in Kineton and its Pony Club has taught generations of young riders the ways of horsemanship, horse care and grooming. In the late 20th century the countryside has come under increasing pressure as land has been taken for new roads, factories and housing, and it is difficult to see at present whether the Warwickshire Hunt will be able to continue its long association with Kineton.

Chapter 4

Village Life

The Mothers' Union and Women's Institute - the Early Years

October 1917 saw the formation in Kineton of two organisations specifically for women - the Mothers' Union and the Women's Institute. Both were a response to the effects of the First World War, offering women the opportunity to meet together on a regular basis and to enjoy the mutual support which we now understand to be so necessary at times of stress. Both were catering for mothers and wives who were desperately anxious about their loved ones at the front. In many cases these women were taking on the whole burden of responsibility for their families for the first time in their lives, and working for the country in a way that had never been expected before. This was as true of those who set up and ran the organisations - like the Lady Willoughby de Broke, Mrs Dora Fielden and the Honourable Mabel Verney - as it was of the ordinary members. Speaking to the **Mothers' Union**, the Hon. Mabel Verney foresaw no conflict of interest between the two organisations; she considered "the Mothers' Union the spiritual side of life and the Women's Institute more the duty towards your neighbour".

At the opening meeting of the **Mothers' Union** its objects were defined as

> 1. To uphold the sanctity of marriage; 2. To awaken in mothers of all classes a sense of their great responsibility in the training of their boys and girls, the future fathers and mothers of the Empire; 3. To organize a band of mothers who will seek by their own example to lead their families in purity and holiness of life, and to reform the morals and raise the tone of this country through their homes, on the principle that education begins at home.

The following week, those attending the first public meeting of the **Women's Institute** heard that

> it was their duty to bring all the land they could under cultivation and produce as much food as possible for the people. Agriculture was the mainspring of all industries, and they must avail themselves of every organisation to build up England on the scale of pre-war times. They must learn to economise, and to store as much produce as possible, so that they might not have to depend on supplies from across the seas. A Woman's Institute was a real social centre for working out the objects they sought to attain.

Kineton: The Village and its History

Members of the Women's Institute enter the 'Shakespearian Competition' in 1925.

Although the Women's Institute movement had begun in Canada in 1897, it was not until September 1915 that the first Institute was opened in Britain. By the beginning of 1917 there were already 40 branches in the country. The Kineton Institute was founded in the September of that year, with its first public meeting in October. Within six months, many practical projects were already under way. A collecting point for locally grown produce to send to markets in the towns was established in the Woodley House stables; more than 1,000 glass preserving jars had been ordered, and the Prime Minister's wife had been asked to use her influence to secure sugar for fruit preservation. A lending library was proposed in 1919, and by joining with the Carnegie Lending Library in 1920 there began a close association with the library service of the County Council that continued for several decades. In 1921, at the same time as the building of a Women's Institute Hall was being considered, a Coal Club was established to provide subscribing members with household coal at reasonable prices. When bad coal was delivered the unfortunate contractor was summoned to appear before the disapproving committee to apologise and offer compensation. The Institute took over the care of the village War Memorial in 1924, establishing its own War Memorial sub-committee and arranging for the building of the retaining wall that still protects it today. This responsibility continued until 1940 when it was transferred to the Women's Branch of the British Legion.

The summer fetes and flower shows held to raise funds for the building of a Women's Institute Hall were so successful that other village organisations, such as the Nursing Association, the Fire Brigade and the Cricket Club, worked hard to be associated with them. With the opening of the W.I. Hall in 1924, Kineton was provided with a long-lasting focus for many of its activities. The men's billiard club had 43 members in 1925. Boxing tournaments were held, although an extra charge of five shillings had to be made to have the Hall cleaned afterwards. During 1934 agreement was reached for the monthly meetings of the Petty Sessional Court to transfer permanently from the Public Hall in Warwick Road to the W.I. Hall. Then, early in 1939, came the first response to the threat of a Second World War with the opening of emergency nursing classes, fee one shilling for six classes.

Throughout the next five years, the members of the Women's Institute and their Hall were central to Kineton's war effort. By late October 1939, within less than two months of the outbreak of war, the Hall was being used as a school for children evacuated from Coventry. A soldiers' mobile canteen soon replaced the school for evacuees, and was followed by a YMCA canteen under the supervision of Lady Willoughby de Broke. Meanwhile, the members were knitting for troops abroad, mending for soldiers stationed in the village, and undertaking a multitude of other tasks in support of the 'war effort'. It was proudly reported (with some precision!) that, in one period of four months, 299lbs of jam and 69 lbs of pickle had been made, 3,420 meat pies sold, and that, between 1939 and 1945, no fewer than 2,939 garments had been made for the Red Cross. After the war, as well as continuing as the focus for a wide range of village activities, the hall was used by the village school for 'school dinners'.

Other women's groups, especially small groups catering for special interests, have, over the years, joined the two veterans. Both the Mothers' Union and the Women's Institute continue to attract new members, and now both meet in the Village Hall which replaced the old W.I. Hall in 1986.

The Brass Band

For much of the 19th century the organisers of Kineton fetes and parades had to hire a brass or silver band from distant towns and villages or, for a really big event, to engage the 'splendid band' of the Warwickshire Yeomanry Cavalry. Then, for a brief period in the 1880s, Kineton had its own brass band. Comments recorded during the relatively short life of this band, (and of its successor, the Kineton Drum and Fife Band), suggest that it was noted more for its enthusiasm than for its musical achievement.

It is not known how or exactly when the Kineton Band was formed. The first mention we can find is in the Parish Magazine for February 1883 and refers to "a rumour of the probability of a speedy breaking up of the Band". Happily this rumour was ill founded, for the magazine was soon able to report that the band had played at several entertainments during the following

Whitsun week, adding the comment: "as perseverance deserves success, we heartily give the members our best wishes." A year later the band launched an appeal for new uniforms, and their enthusiasm was rewarded. It had gained them the support of the local nobility, gentry and tradesmen, who, within a month, had subscribed enough money to allow the band to show off their new uniforms and instruments in a parade through Kineton. The Stratford Herald reported that:

> the order for supplying it was given to Mr W H Wilkins, tailor, of Kineton, who has given great satisfaction in the execution of the order. The uniform is composed of dark blue serge, braided with yellow. It is effective, but neat. The band has improved very much in their playing.

The Parish Magazine was more cautious. Whilst conceding that "The old uniform was decidedly too showy in appearance, and we think the Band have this time shewn better discretion in selecting a more neat and less conspicuous facings and colour," the correspondent felt

> The Band has certainly a great difficulty to contend with, namely, the want of an efficient instructor. The advice we would give them is this: "Get someone to have the perfect control of the whole arrangements of the Band, whose word shall be law".

The Kineton band was not popular with everyone. In December 1884 the Parish Magazine fought back at "those who exclaim 'Kineton needs no band' ", saying

> if in a small town like this, only one or two young men are benefited either in moral or intellectual advancement or in being preserved from any kind of temptation, surely a good work has then been done by providing them with pleasant occupation or amusement for their leisure. For these reasons we are gratified at the Kineton band still existing.

Despite its apparent shortcomings, the Kineton Brass Band was still in existence in June 1887 when it took part in the celebration of the Golden Jubilee of Queen Victoria's reign and headed the procession from the parish church to the grounds of Kineton House (now Norton Grange). Six months later, its place in people's affections had been taken by the Kineton Drum and Fife Band, and the Parish Magazine expressed the rather forlorn hope that "this new band will continue, and not suddenly fall away as the brass band has done." The new band did continue long enough to play at the Combroke Village Wake in July 1888 to such success that the villagers there "very much wish we saw our way to starting a Drum and Fife Band in Combroke."

Regrettably it would seem that the encouragement shown by the Parish Magazine was overtaken by changing fashions in music, and reports of Kineton's band appear less frequently.

Celebrating May Day

May Day was originally a pagan festival celebrating the arrival of spring, although many of the activities now associated with it originated in Victorian times. The log books kept by the head teachers of the church school give some idea of how the first day of May was marked in Kineton during the late 19th and early 20th centuries.

During the 1870s it was the custom to practice May Day songs on several mornings in late April, to close early on 30 April to allow the children to gather flowers for their May Pole, and to grant a holiday the next day when the May Pole would be carried around the village. Teachers in later years may have been less enthusiastic, but they had to record "Many children absent today picking cowslips and going round with May garlands" and "Owing to it being the First of May there was a poor attendance this morning."

Early in the 20th century, 24 May was designated Empire Day as a way of encouraging schoolchildren to be aware of their duties and responsibilities as citizens of the British Empire. An entry in the school log for 1908 records

> Today by order of the County Council lessons on 'The Empire' were given in the morning concluding with the singing of The Flag of Britain - when the flag was saluted - and the National Anthem.

At the same time the revival of interest in English folk song and dance was matched by the enthusiasm of Joseph Chandler, headmaster for thirty-nine years, who soon combined the May

Schoolchildren take the Maypole round the village.

Day celebrations with Empire Day in colourful displays of song and dance. The following report comes from 1918.

> May Day and Empire Day were commemorated on an imposing scale on Friday last. The May Queen (Annie Bubb) was supported by four maids of honour, twelve Morris dancers, six girls in pink and blue, six boys in smocks, Jack-o'-the-Green (Harry Wisdom), six sweeps, the hobby horse (Reggie Edden), the fool (Charles Newbold), and a band of maypole dancers. The Empire was represented by a Herald (Lewis Smart) carrying a Union Jack, England by Ethel Baldwin, Scotland by Jessie Robertson, and Ireland by Thomas Wisdom. India, South Africa, Australia, New Zealand, Canada, and Newfoundland also had suitable representatives. Several other children carried flags and flowers, and a prettily-decorated miniature maypole was in charge of twelve infants. The children met at the school at nine o'clock, and paraded the town till 12.30, giving en route maypole and other dances. On returning to the playground the May Queen was crowned by the Rev C Jickling, who congratulated Mr Chandler and the teachers on the excellent programme they had provided. In reply, Mr Chandler assured the company that it had given the children, the teachers, and himself great pleasure to arrange the celebration, and he thanked all for their generous response to the appeal for contributions to the National Egg collection for Wounded Soldiers. In the evening the children gave another performance on the Green in Southam-street, and this was followed by dancing for adults, Mr Chandler providing violin music. A happy day was brought to a close at eight o'clock by the singing of the Empire Song and the National Anthem. The collection amounted to £8 7s 6d.

The Salvation Army

The Salvation Army was founded by William Booth in 1865 and was organised along military lines for Christian evangelism and social work among the poor of London. Its activities soon spread beyond the capital. When the Army held an open-air meeting on Edge Hill in July 1882 more than 200 people attended, probably because the rumour got about that a second Battle of Edge Hill was expected to take place, for which 10,000 volunteers were wanted.

A permanent presence was established in Kineton six years later with the arrival of two officers, who opened a small meeting-place in Banbury Street. After their initial campaign, which began in March 1888, the officers' experience of Kineton was reported in the nationally distributed 'War Cry', as shown on the next page, complete with idiosyncratic layout.

The Army continued to be active in Kineton for another two years and must have established good relations with the villagers for, in its report of the funeral of the Anglican vicar in January 1890, the Stratford Herald noted that a "good number of the Salvation Army were also present as one of the last marks of respect to the memory of their departed friend." In April, on the

> **A Bundle of KINETON'S 'Queer Sticks'**
>
> A glorious ten weeks' campaign. Real old-fashioned trophies.
>
> Any one who doubts whether The Army is still doing the work it used to do should ask somebody who knows.
>
> 'Somebody who knows' is Captain Kirkup, of Kineton, whose glorious record since a little over two months ago is,
>
> Seventy souls in ten weeks;
>
> all of whom, with the exception of three, are still going forward.
>
> Among these are some real gems, dug from the pit.
>
> No.1 could not say three words without swearing, now he says God has given him a new tongue.
>
> No.2 is a young man well brought up, who had drunk himself into poverty. God took hold of him the first meeting he came to. After three weeks holding out he surrendered. Once, he says, his motto was 'Anything for a bit of devilry', now it is 'Anything for Jesus'.
>
> No.3 was once possessed by the spirit of stubbornness, so that he would come home drunk and sit up all night to spite his mother if she asked him to go to bed. He is now ready, he says, to go to Stafford Jail, or anywhere else for Jesus.

Extract from the 'War Cry'

third anniversary of the Army's arrival, there was a general parade and marching through the streets accompanied by the brass band, open air services were held, and addresses were delivered in the Liberal club-room packed to overflowing. Then things appear to have declined rapidly. By July, the Stratford Herald was reporting rather cynically that when the Army paraded with its band round the village on Sunday "they ceased playing when near to the public places of worship, which certainly gave considerable satisfaction to more than a few of the inhabitants of the place." During the same month the garden of the resident officers was vandalised and, in November, only four months after a change of officers, the Salvation Army had left Kineton. The Stratford Herald recorded "the army here, which was some little time ago fairly well recruited, is now quite disbanded, and for the present, at any rate, it is only to be remembered as one amongst many other things of the past in Kineton."

Some Church Choir Outings   1891 - 1914

The arrival of the Rev Arthur Watson at St Peter's Church in 1890 gave new life to the choir. He was ably assisted in this work by the young Guernsey Walsingham Webb, headmaster of the Middle School, who was organist and choirmaster. As a reward for regular attendance at practices and the several services each Sunday, the men and boys of the choir were offered an annual outing to a place of interest. Thirty-two members of the choir went on the first outing - to the Warwickshire Agricultural Show at Alcester. This modest outing lasted only twelve hours. The next trip lasted more than sixteen hours, with the choir members attending divine service in Oxford and visiting the colleges in the morning before spending three and a half hours cruising on the Thames. The elements to be found in nearly all future outings until the Great War had been established - long hours spent away from Kineton, several of them on the train, and instruction mixed with recreation.

Indeed, by 1897, time and distance no longer seemed to matter.

> On Monday upwards of 30 members of the choir, accompanied by the vicar, had their annual treat, starting at 2 am in wagonettes to meet the excursion at Harbury Station en route for Folkestone and Dover. After an enjoyable journey they reached Dover at 10 a.m.; here they followed their own inclinations until one o'clock, the hour for dinner. Having satisfied the inner man and done ample justice to all the

St Peter's Church choir in 1892.

good things supplied, the different parties explored the various objects of interest in the neighbourhood, and a very jolly time was spent. But it was found as the train was starting that one boy was missing, one who was conspicuous by the absence of an arm, which led to his identification, and for once proved a blessing to him; but owing to the thoughtfulness of the Vicar, who telegraphed, he was sent on the next train, and joined the party at Folkestone. All reached their destination at four o'clock on Tuesday morning, thoroughly well satisfied with their holiday.

The choir was in Barmouth on the Welsh coast in 1899, and by 1907 the annual outing had reached Cleethorpes "the attractive sea-side resort on the North Lincolnshire coast, in close proximity with Grimsby, England's greatest fish port" where "nearly three most instructive hours were spent inspecting the docks and fish market." The next year they went to the Franco-British Exhibition in Shepherds Bush and some brave soul drew attention to the "quick and comfortable journey to London, much to be preferred to the weary hours often spent in the train." To no avail; in 1909 they went to Llandudno where "in spite of a very long journey, an enjoyable day was spent" and to Great Yarmouth in 1910.

Life was less strenuous for the choir after the Great War. Motor coaches replaced the train, while Coventry and Oxford provided sufficient excitement for a day's outing.

Kineton Flower Shows

Kineton can still boast a Gardening Club and an annual Flower and Produce Show. Although neither of these organisations is a direct descendant of the Horticultural and Floricultural Society established in 1860, they belong to a tradition started at that time and continued in the well-remembered Flower Shows and Fetes organised by the Women's Institute between the World Wars.

The original society was formed "to encourage a taste for useful and ornamental gardening in Kineton and the neighbouring parishes". Their first show was held in a field in Little Kineton on 2 August 1861, complete with a large marquee, refreshment tents, and the band of the First Warwickshire Militia. The following year, there were six marquees and it was estimated that two thousand people attended; at dusk, Mr Edwin Tucker, a pyrotechnic artist from the Royal Cremorne Gardens, displayed a variety of fireworks, "which were very beautiful and gave every satisfaction".

The following descriptions of the twelfth show held in 1873, taken from a contemporary report in the Warwick Advertiser, give some idea of Kineton's pre-eminent position at that time.

> The Annual Show of the Kineton Horticultural Society was held on Wednesday last (13th August). The tents, through the kindness of Georgiana Lady Willoughby de Broke, were again pitched in the grounds of Kineton House, from which there is a beautiful view of the bold range of Edge Hills, and the valley where the

memorable battle was fought. Kineton Flower Show yields to no rural show in Warwickshire; and the last exhibition was the most successful ever held. This result was in no small degree owing to the opening of the line of railway from Kineton to Stratford [only six weeks earlier]. Special excursion tickets were issued; and a large number of Stratford people took the opportunity of enjoying a glance at the new line and paying a visit to the Kineton Show. The long line of vehicles in the village reminded one of a London thoroughfare, or a busy market town, and showed that old modes of travelling are still indispensable. About 3,000 persons visited the show. The weather was all that either committee or visitors could desire. The only thing that in any sense mars a flower-show is the simple fact that all exhibitors cannot be high prize winners; and the decorated arch over the gateway, with its rhyming legend "He who never tries cannot hope to gain a prize" showed as much thoughtful consideration in the conception of the idea as artistic skill in its execution. The park roadway was gaily decorated; and from the boughs of the old elms near the show were suspended Chinese lanterns, which were, later in the evening, illuminated.

The band of the Warwickshire Yeomanry Cavalry was in attendance, and played an excellent selection of operatic and dance music. We believe that the providing of an excellent tea at a very moderate sum contributes no little to the success of the Kineton show. Undoubtedly the society owes much to the fostering care of Lord Willoughby. Horticultural taste seems hereditary at Compton Verney, and it is pleasing to find that the old traditions are so well maintained.

As night approached, the fairy-like forms of those who were dancing to the lively music of the Yeomanry band, the festoons and garlands, the shadows playing on the weather-beaten trunk and leafy bough, made up a pretty picture and, later in the evening, the glittering lights transformed the whole scene in the most bewitching manner.

Perhaps some of that large scale and varied entertainment will return to Kineton's Flower Shows in the twenty-first century.

Kyneton, Australia

On a wall in the Village Hall is a plaque with a map of the Australian continent and a shield showing the arms of the Shire of Kyneton, Australia. It was given to the Parish Council as a reminder of the long association between the village of Kineton, Warwickshire, and the township of Kyneton, Australia.

Kyneton, with a population of about 5000, lies on the Campaspe River, about 50 miles north-west of Melbourne, the state capital of Victoria. During the goldrush of the 1850s and 60s it turned from a small settlement into a thriving town because it was on the direct route to the goldfields. The opening of the Melbourne to Bendigo railway through Kyneton in 1862 helped it to survive after the goldrush by providing reliable transport for its market garden produce to the city. Today the main industries of Kyneton include agriculture, abattoirs, knitting and timber mills, wineries, foundries, and a growing tourist industry. In 1998 it celebrated 150 years since its selection as a township.

The traditional story of the connection between a Warwickshire village and the Australian outback was told in a 1953 edition of the Kyneton Guardian and was reprinted in the Echo, Kineton's local newspaper

> At a meeting of the settlers to select a town site, Mr. LaTrobe [superintendent of the District] gave Mrs. Jeffreys [mother of one of the established settlers] the privilege of naming the new town site. She suggested the name of her native town in Warwickshire, England - Kineton - but this was modified to Kyneton, meaning the town at the back of the wood.

Little is known of the origins of Mrs Juliana Jeffreys, and it has not yet been possible to confirm her association with Kineton, Warwickshire. Indeed, a more recent article in the Kyneton Guardian suggests that Mrs Jeffreys was Irish and that her husband came from Kington, previously Kyneton, in Herefordshire. The newspaper did, however, have the grace to conclude the article "Does that end all arguments? You can bet it doesn't."

Whatever the outcome, over the years there have been many attempts to foster relationships between the two communities. In 1927 the Rector of St Paul's Church, Kyneton, wrote to Canon Holbech in Kineton proposing a year-long exchange of parishes, and his parish magazine reported that

> a suggestion has gone forth that it might be possible to secure a stone from the Church in Kineton to build into our new Tower, thus symbolising our undivided unity, and of the wish to build into our Australian life all that is highest and best from the old Mother land.

Shortages at the end of the Second World War brought offers of food parcels from Kyneton. In 1948, following a proposal from the Kyneton Country Women's Guild that the two groups should exchange ideas, the Kineton Women's Institute agreed that a different member should write to Australia after each meeting. Good relationships must have been established, for in 1952 the Stratford Herald reported a visit by the Kyneton president to the Kineton W I and commented that "The two organisations have corresponded for many years". Another approach was made by a former Kineton farmer who moved to Kyneton, Australia in 1953. He hoped to establish a link between the two football teams, and presented the Kineton Wasps with an autographed football.

More recently other Kyneton residents have visited the village with the aim of linking the two communities. Certainly great interest was shown in reports of the 150th anniversary celebrations in Kyneton, and whatever historical evidence may come to light in the future, it seems unlikely that the connection will now be broken.

Kineton from 'Big Field'. An unusual view showing the long-demolished cottages by the River Dene

Kineton - My Village
by Walter Hartless (b.1908)

Walter Hartless has lived in Kineton since he was three years of age. This poem, written in the 1970s, recalls the people who lived in the village just after the end of the First World War. Some of them, like the Honourable Mabel Verney and Ernest Parke J P, were people whose importance extended beyond Kineton itself, but, typically, only those features which stick in a child's memory are mentioned, and all villagers appear as equals.

> I remember Kineton when a man's word was his bond
> And the moorhen dared to build its nest
> On Peg Leg Pollard's pond.
> When Park Piece *was* a peaceful park,
> A home for song thrush, finch and lark.
> And rooks and crows made their abode
> In the elms that bordered Warwick Road.

Village Life

I remember when it was the rule
That children went to Sunday School,
And often in St Peter's Church
For an empty pew one had to search.
There were no ladies in the choir
For the stalls were filled with son and sire;
When Miss May Webb the organ thumped,
And Albert Collett pumped and pumped.

I remember when the River Dene
Flowed through the village, swift and clean,
A paradise for boys with boats,
And fishing rods with bobbing floats.
And the kingfisher, a brilliant blue,
Very often came in view.
But now it's just a rubbish dump
Choked with weed and willow stump.

I also can remember well,
When the fire alarm was the old church bell.
They had no engine then, of course,
So the motive power was Faulkner's horse.
There was Franklin, Freeman, Alsop, Pett,
Wisdom, Rawlins, Green, Collett.
They really were a gallant band
With Tubby Coles in full command.
And their devotion to duty was never in doubt,
But when they arrived at a fire, it was usually out!

I remember Town Crier Shepherd with his bell and silk top hat;
Quaker Parkes, Gunner Bates and Boer War Bugler Bratt;
Schoolmaster Joey Chandler with his beard a ginger red;
And dear Miss Ada Bloxham, who used to bake our bread.
Scoutmaster George Orme Tiley with his famous boxing eight,
Admiral Cowan, Miss Mabel Verney, also Danny Thwaite.
What memories these names recall
Of Kineton when its folk walked tall!

Chapter 5
A Reference File for Researchers

Local History relies on the collection of small amounts of information from a great number of sources. Even in compiling a brief history such as this it has been necessary to refer to a wide number of documents, and to make an attempt to verify the 'folk' memory of the community. Most of our sources are to be found within easy travelling distance of Kineton, in the two local record offices - the Warwickshire County Record Office (WCRO) at Priory Park in Warwick and the Shakespeare Birthplace Trust Records Office (SBTRO) in Henley Street, Stratford-upon-Avon - and in the larger libraries in Leamington, Stratford and Warwick. Many of the books and papers quoted can be consulted in most, if not all, of these places. Their staff have been most encouraging, and are pleased to help with any enquiries.

For those who want to know more, there is a great deal of material as yet unexplored, and the following notes may be helpful as a pointer as to where to look.

General Interest

Victoria County History

The Victoria County History for Warwickshire was published in eight large volumes in a period spanning the first half of the 20th century. The main description of Kineton's history can be found in pages 103-108 of volume 5, which was published in 1949. The article includes information about the growth of the village, the manors, the churches and the charities for the poor. It also contains many references for further reading.

Census Returns 1821-1891

A census of the whole country has been held every 10 years since 1801, except in 1941 during the Second World War. Although little of the material from censuses before 1841 survives nationally, there is a book of census returns for Kineton in 1821 [WCRO, DR 212/194] From 1841 onwards the returns have become increasingly more comprehensive. To maintain the confidential nature of the replies to the enumerator's questions the detailed lists are released only after 100 years have elapsed, and so the 1891 census is the latest currently available. By 1891 the information for each household included the name and surname of everyone at that residence on census night, together with their age, relationship to the head of the family, marital status, occupation, and place of birth. Summary tables of population and household size, age and occupational analyses, etc., are available from later censuses, but do not give any details for individuals. The census returns are easy to use, on microfilm and increasingly on CD-ROM, and are sometimes indexed.

Parish Registers

The Parish Registers contain entries for baptisms, marriages and burials, and are an important source of information for anyone tracing the history of a family. The registers for St Peter's Church, Kineton, not currently in use are held in the Warwick County Record Office and cover the following periods:- Baptisms 1546-1952, Marriages 1539-1971, Burials 1577-1906.

There is also a record of baptisms for the Kineton Methodist Circuit 1843-1951 [WCRO, CR 2332]. Some details of the membership of the Independent Chapel in Little Kineton can be found in a minute book covering the period 1813-1882. [WCRO, CR 984/4]

Other Parish Records

During the 16th and 17th centuries the Parish Vestry, comprising the vicar, churchwardens and leading parishioners, took over many of the old functions of the Manor Court. By the 1850s the Kineton Vestry was appointing annually two churchwardens, two overseers of the poor, two assessors of taxes, and separate surveyors of the highways for Great and Little Kineton, as well as nominating two guardians to serve on the Board of Guardians for the management of poor relief through the Stratford Union. Vestry minute books from 1809 onwards, together with account and rate books for the surveyors of the highways and the overseers of the poor, provide detailed information about the running of the village in the 19th century [WCRO, DR 212]. The workings of the poor law and its effects on individuals and families are particularly well documented in a packet of 104 pieces of the overseers' correspondence between 1807 and 1836 [WCRO, DR 212/111] ; this contains not only the official communications with other parishes but also the revealing pleas and demands for help from the poor themselves.

Trade Directories

Trade directories are an easily accessible source of information about towns and villages in the Victorian and Edwardian period. Entries usually begin with a brief outline of the history and topography of the village, with some reference to recent events, for example the closure of the market or the opening of the railway station. This is followed by lists of the principal inhabitants and of the various professional, business and trades people. The lists are not comprehensive and, unlike the census, do not record labourers, domestic servants, and other employees.

The earliest entry for Kineton is in Pigot's Warwickshire directory for 1828/9 ; similar entries can be found in his directories for 1830, 1835 and 1841. From 1844 onwards these directories appeared under the name of Slater, and were later absorbed into the famous Kelly's directories which continued to print entries for Kineton until 1940. There are also entries for Kineton in White's directories for 1850 and 1874. From the 1880s until 1927, the most complete lists of heads of households arranged by name, by street and by trade are to be found in the annual directories of Robert Spennell, a Warwick publisher.

Local Newspapers

Extensive use can be made of items in local newspapers and the Parish Magazine to find details of 19th and early 20th century life. Whether or not a particular event is reported in the newspaper is very much dependent on the interests of the local correspondent of the time, and the quantity and quality of the Kineton news varies from year to year. The advertising pages of newspapers can be a fruitful source of information on property and trade sales, as well providing information about forthcoming events such as the Kineton Flower Show or the opening of a school. The Records Office in Stratford is currently compiling an index to the Stratford Herald.

Newspapers covering the Kineton area include the Warwick Advertiser (started 1806), the Leamington Courier (started 1828), the Rugby Advertiser (started 1846), the Stratford Herald (started 1860, first Kineton report 1866), and the Banbury Guardian. The record offices and main libraries will be able to advise on the whereabouts of the various titles, which are often available only on microfilm.

Kineton news can also be found in the eighteen editions of a local newspaper 'The Echo', published by Gordon Norwood and the Roundwood Press between 4 November 1952 and 2 March 1954. [WCRO, MI 430]

The Parish Magazine, covering several of the surrounding parishes as well as Kineton itself, first appeared in 1883. The monthly entry for Kineton did not confine itself to a record of church matters and often contained a lot of interesting (and often amusing) descriptions of village life and activities. [WCRO, DR220/34 onwards].

Warwickshire Museums Service

For non-documentary evidence of the history and development of the Kineton area it is well worth visiting the Warwickshire Museum in Warwick and, in particular, consulting the Warwickshire Sites and Monuments Record which contains information on archaeological sites and finds together with an air photograph collection.

Specific Interest

The Saxon Charter

The gift of 10 hides of land in Kineton (1 hide was normally 120 acres) from King Edgar to his thegn Aelfwold is described in a surviving charter of AD 969, the Saxon period. It is useful both because it shows that Kineton was in the ownership of the King as early as AD 969 and also because it defines the boundaries of his gift. The full version is given in *Cartularium Saxonicum*, volume 3, ed. Birch (London:1893)

The document, some of which is in Latin and some in Anglo-Saxon, describes a stream called the 'Welesburnan', presumably now called the River Dene, and a ditch by 'the paved road', almost certainly the ditch, or 'fosse' which was a frontier boundary and which gave its name to the paved Roman Fosse Way. Other locations are more obscure, but may include a reference to the original, possibly stagnant, water at Combroke, which was adapted by Capability Brown in 1770 to make the Compton Verney lakes, and to the hill leading up from Compton Verney towards Kineton. The Mercian boundary is also mentioned.

It would therefore seem that the king's gift contained much of the present parishes of Kineton and Combroke, but excluded a large tract of land south of the River Dene between the Banbury Road and the Red Road.

Domesday Book

Kineton is one of only nine locations in Warwickshire listed in the Domesday Book of AD 1086 as belonging directly to the King. Originally written in Latin, a modern translation of the entry reads

> The King holds in Fexhole Hundred
> Quintone and Waleborne. King Edward (the Confessor) held them. 3 hides. Land for...
> In lordship 6 ploughs; 3 male and 2 female slaves;
> 100 villagers less 7 and 18 smallholders with 32 ploughs.
> Meadow, 130 acres; woodland ½ league and 2 furlongs long and 4 furlongs wide.
> This is the manor and the outlier together.[†]

One fascinating aspect of this entry is the size of the holding, only 3 hides instead of the 10 hides described by the Saxon Charter. Either the entry was wrong or else the Normans had not yet taken the land from the Saxons.

The Enclosure Awards [WCRO. Kineton Magna, DR 212/179; Kineton Parva, DR 212/178, probably originals. Also several copies, especially at QS 75/64 and QS 75/65]

In the 18th century the two Enclosure Awards affecting Kineton were made : the first, in 1733, was for the Manor of Kineton Parva, and Kineton Magna followed in 1792. The Awards defined not only land ownership but also the public carriageways, private roads and footpaths, thereby creating the legal basis on which many rights of way are now judged.

There is no map attached to either enclosure award in the Warwickshire Record Office, so it requires detailed work with a modern map to attempt to reconstruct the details of the awards. Such work confirms that the pattern of fields and roads determined more than two hundred years ago is much the same today.

The 1774 Survey of Kineton Magna [SBTRO, DR 636/42]

In 1774 the Agent to the Earl of Warwick, who was then the Lord of the Manor of Kineton Magna, produced a survey of the property and land owned by the Earl in Kineton. This survey listed, by streets, "what each copyholder holds and where premises are situate" together with his or her occupation, the annual rent paid, whether any land was rented in the Common Fields, and, most revealingly, who their neighbours were. A typical entry reads

> Barnabas Horseman, Esq., - A messuage and appurtenances in Bridge Street called The Red Lyon. The road leading to Warwick on the North side and a copyhold messuage and appurtenances belonging to William Woodley, Officer of Excise and

---

[†] Reproduced by kind permission from the Phillimore edition of DOMESDAY BOOK (General Editor John Morris), volume 23 Warwickshire, (County Editor Judy Plaister) published in 1976 by Phillimore & Co Ltd, Shopwyke Manor Barn, Chichester, West Sussex.

clock maker, on the South side and two yard lands belonging to the said Barnabas Horseman in the Common Fields of Great Kington. £0-15-5d.

As the survey covered all the streets in Kineton Magna, it is possible to work out the detailed layout of the houses in the village in 1774, though this task is by no means as simple as it sounds.

Manorial Court Rolls

The proceedings of manorial courts, rejoicing in the names of 'Courts Leet with View of Frankpledge' and 'Courts Baron', are recorded in court rolls. The more accessible records are, in fact, to be found in book form, although until 1733 they were normally written in Latin. Among other matters, these courts dealt with the transfer of copyhold land upon inheritance or sale and a fairly complete picture of who lived where can be built up from the changes of tenancy shown in the court rolls. The surviving records for Kineton and Little Kineton, covering much of the period from the 15th to the 20th century, are distributed between the two Record Offices.

Church Sittings book

Another interesting document, which supplements information from the 1774 Survey and the Manorial Court Rolls, is the Church Sittings Book [WCRO, DR 212/38]. According to the introduction this record "was copied from a book belonging to Mr Johns - which was taken by him from an old book now in the possession of the Vicar of Kineton made at the time the Church was built in 1755. The explanation on the right hand pages was made out by the Churchwardens in 1821." It lists the properties to which pews in the parish church belonged in 1755 and 1821, with some additional changes in 1836, and also gives some indication of the occupation or trade of the owners.

The Account Book of George Lines

George Lines died in 1899 at the age of 72. His early years were spent at Battle Farm (now part of DM Kineton). After the death of his father in 1851, he gave up farming to become licensee of the Swan Inn in Kineton for more than twenty years. In later life he undertook many varied tasks, including assistant overseer of the poor, rate collector, secretary to the Kineton Gas Company, and first clerk of the Parish Council in 1894.

The book that bears his name [WCRO, CR 3222] is much more than a series of farm accounts, although it does provide a detailed picture of farming costs and practices in the 1840s. It is also a diary of local and national events, for example

    1850   9 July   Funeral of Sir Robert Peel
              12 July Began mowing
              15 July The price of wheat is about 16 shillings to sixteen shillings and sixpence
              17 July Balloon ascended from Leamington.

It also includes a record of special events held at the Swan Inn, including menus and recipes, a scrapbook of press cuttings; and jottings relating to his public work.

Other Published Work.

Miller, George. ***Rambles Round the Edge Hills***, **first published 1896. Reprinted edition Roundwood Press, Kineton, 1975. ISBN 0 900093 58 7**

Titchmarsh, Peter. *The Parish Church of St Peter, Kineton, Warwickshire,* Kineton PCC, 1983

Gill, David. *The Kineton Methodists 1842-1993,* Kineton 1993

Ashley-Smith, Gillian. *Kineton in the Great War 1914-1921,* Brewin Books, Studley, 1998. ISBN 1 85858 111 7

INDEX

1774 survey	7, 36, 37, 44, 64
Admiral's House	23
Aelfwold	2
Arch, Joseph	40
Aylworth, Francis	24, 58
Aylworth, Thomas	67
Baker, Fred, baker	27
Ballard's bread	67
Banbury Street	26-31
Bancroft family, chemists	26
Bank House	26
Benfield, Kenneth	59
Bentley family	6, 17, 52, 59
Berkeley family	58
Big Field	30, 51
Blunt, Caroline	40, 69
Box Tree Cottage	41
Brass Band	91-2
Brewer, J Selmin	71
Brickworks	64
Bridge Street	17-23
Brisker family, builders	36
Brookhampton	1, 4, 49
Burgoyne, Robert	5
Burton, William	58
Cemetery	43
Central Stores	34
Chadshunt	6
Chandler, Joseph	70, 79, 93
Charter	
- Saxon	1, 104
- Markets and fairs	3, 39
Churches	
- Independent	9, 53
- Methodist	9, 37
- Salvation Army	94-5
- St Francis RC	19, 36
- St Peter's CE	2, 4, 15-16
Church Choir	96
Church	
- Bells	15
- Clock	15
- Weathervane	15
Church Houses	24
Church Well	30
Cinema	34
Clarendon House	22-3, 73
Clockmaker's Cottage	43
Clubs	
- Conservative Working Men	35
- Liberal	34
- Sports and Social	51-2
Coffee House	42
Coles, William E	28, 75, 81
Compton Verney House	12, 14, 50, 59, 78
Copyhold	57
Corn Mill	33, 81
Court family, glaziers	23
Court House	18
Cowan, Admiral Sir Walter	16, 44
Craddocks	29
Cricket	29, 51
Czech soldiers	12, 45
Dene House	21
Diana Lodge	55, 72
DM Kineton	13, 55
Dodson, GE	73
Domesday book	2, 10, 105
Duckett, Charles	28
Edgehill, Battle of	5, 13, 32
Edmunds, Barbara	72
Electricity	11
Enclosures	8, 30, 50, 105
Feldon	1, 59
Fielden, Joshua	11, 51, 53, 88

Index

Fighting Close	43
Fire Brigade	41, 46, 74-6
Fisher, Joseph	19
Flower shows	97-8
Football Clubs	
- Albion	52
- United	19, 51
- Wasps	52
Forge House	37, 38
Fox Cottage	41, 59
Fyfe Lodge	36
Garrett, Thomas	20, 25
Gas Company	9, 46, 66, 77-9
Green Farm End	33
Greenhill's Stores	28
Griffin, George	21, 29, 79
Griffin, Thomas	44
Grimes, Samuel P	30
Hanbury, Hon Patience	23, 44
Hartless, Walter	100
Haven House	45
Heronwood House	29
Hill, Richard	52
Hog Lane	18
Hundred	3
Hunt, Charles	85
Hunter, James	72
Independents	9, 53
Inns	64-5
- Carpenter's Arms	28, 65
- Drum and Monkey	65
- New	42, 65
- Railway	29, 65
- Red Lion	19, 25, 65
- Rose and Crown	40, 65
- Swan	25, 65
- Woolpack	29, 65
Johns, William	66, 69, 71
Jurassic Way	1
Kenilworth Priory	2, 6, 15, 24, 58
Kineton Garage	44
Kineton Green Buses	11, 85-6
Kineton House	11, 12, 52, 97
Kineton Medal	6
King Charles I	5, 6
King Edgar	1
King John	3, 47, 49, 56
King John's Mound	3, 47
King John's Well	49
King, Bolton	34, 35
Kyneton, Australia	98-9
Land girls	12, 27
Lewis family, butchers	25
Library	45
Lines family	62
Lines, George	67, 79, 106
Little Kineton Mansion	58
Little Kineton	51-5
Lucas factory	12
Manor House	23
Manor Lane	18
Manor, Lords of	36, 44, 56, 57, 60
Markets	3, 9, 19, 39, 43, 62
Market Square	39-42
May Day	93-4
Middleton, Captain WG	87
Midland Bank	29
Milepost	49
Millenium Wood	50
Miller, Rev Francis	16, 36, 41, 69
Miller, Sanderson	7, 15
Mothers' Union	89
Mowbray, Thomas	4, 58
Nadbury Camp	1
Naughty Boys Cage	16, 43
North, Lord	18
Norton Grange	11, 12, 52, 59
Norwood, Gordon	21, 27
Oddfellows' cottages	37
Orme Tiley, George	79
Osier beds	30-1
Overseers of the Poor	66
Parish Vestry	66
Petty Sessions	18, 25, 44

Pig Club	63	Talbot, Rev William	15, 24
Pittern Hill	30, 59, 61, 80	Tucker, George	69
Point-to-Point Races	87	Turnpikes	8
Police Station	45		
Population	2, 10, 13	VAD hospital	11, 17, 51
Post Office	20, 29	Verney, Hon Mabel	29, 55, 71
Public Hall	44	Village Hall	34
Public Houses	see Inns	Volunteer Fire Brigade	74-6
Pump	30	Wade family, clockmakers	43
		Walker family, blacksmiths	38
Railway	9, 13, 43, 48, 82-3	Walton House	23
Rawlins, William	24, 29, 31	War Ag Exec Committee	63
Red Road	55, 61	War Memorial	11, 13, 24
River crossings	30, 51	Warwick Road	44-50
River Dene	30, 51	Warwickshire Hunt	9, 10, 53, 62,65, 83, 86-8, 105
Roman Villa	1, 49		
Romano-British Settlement	1, 32	Watson, Rev A	96
Roundheads	51	Webb, Guernsey W	22, 73, 96
Roundwood Press	21	Welchman, Dr Edward	18
Rouse, Arthur	28, 81	Wells, Dr Clement	22
Roxburgh House	45	Wilkins, William H	21
		Williams, Hugh	24, 86
Salvation Army	94-5	Willoughby de Broke family	9, 53, 59, 65
School buildings	40, 41, 42	Willoughby de Broke,	
Schools		16th	23, 52, 69
- Brewer's	71	17th	55, 86
- CE Primary	71	18th	40, 45, 46, 51, 57, 78, 83, 87
- Commercial Academy	71	19th	51, 54, 84, 88
- High	32, 71	20th	41, 43
- Ladies	72	Georgiana	42, 45, 73, 97
- Littledale	73	Marie	89
- Lodge	72	Rachel	34, 91
- Manor Lane	73	Wilson, William	78
- Middle	45, 73	Windmill	50, 79, 80
- National	69-71	Winger, James	71
Segrave, Stephen de	3, 39, 58	Wisdom, Martin	30, 64
Shepherd, Jo	64	Women's Institute Hall	12, 34
Shortacres	32, 33	Women's Institute	89-91, 99
Smart, Lewis, dairyman	33	Woodfields	37
Southam Street	34-8, 42-4	Woodley House	45, 59
Stage coaches	8, 19	Woodley, Josiah	44, 45, 67-8, 79
Street-lighting	79	Woodley, William, clockmaker	65
Sumner, Francis	19, 21	World Wars	10, 11, 12, 22-3, 30
Swine Street	18		